Shakespeare's Life and Times

Shakespeare's Life and Times

A PICTORIAL RECORD

By Roland Mushat Frye

PRINCETON, NEW JERSEY

PRINCETON UNIVERSITY PRESS

To my son,

who taught me to love fishing,

and whom I taught to love Shakespeare

CONTENTS

PREFACE

MORE biographical information is available on William Shakespeare than on almost any other writer of his own age. Most of this information is conveniently assembled in Sir Edmund K. Chambers' *William Shakespeare: A Study of Facts and Problems,* published by the Oxford University Press in 1930. This two-volume work, totaling over one thousand pages, is not a loose narrative, but is packed with documentary and factual evidence and the careful analysis of that evidence. Since Chambers assembled his materials, other scholars have corrected and expanded his work. Despite the weight of this evidence, we still encounter the erroneous cliché that little is known about Shakespeare and his life.

The purpose of my brief biography is to convey as vivid an impression of Shakespeare's life as we can now create on the basis of the available evidence. The hope of conveying a vivid impression should not, however, be interpreted to mean that this is a speculative biography: what the most responsible historical scholarship accepts as fact is stated without qualification here, and what is probable is carefully labeled as such, while mere possibilities are appropriately qualified.

What will be new to most readers is the extensive use of pictures to illustrate and vitalize the bare facts of Shakespeare's life. In addition to authentic pictures of Shakespeare himself, I have included illustrations of baptisms and burials, London and Stratford scenes, everyday activities, and theatrical places or events, as well as portraits of Shakespeare's friends and associates. The majority of these pictures are taken from sixteenth- and seventeenth-century originals, so as to bring Shakespeare to life within the context of his own age. Some photographs and drawings or models made in more recent times have also been included, however, because they represent the most reliable views we have of buildings and scenes of Shakespeare's time. This "pictorial documentation" will, I hope, add a sense of immediacy to the narration and give readers the opportunity to visualize the original events and even to participate imaginatively in them.

The combination of narrative and pictures may dramatize for us the facts of Shakespeare's life and times, but if we are to understand his genius, it can only be by turning to his own works. I hope, however, that this biography will bring us closer to the man who wrote those works.

ROLAND MUSHAT FRYE

The University of Pennsylvania
October 1966

ACKNOWLEDGMENTS

THE acknowledgment of one's gratitude for assistance rendered is one of the more pleasant parts of preparing a book for publication, and in this book I have more than the usual number of thanks to express.

The major debt of gratitude is due to the Folger Shakespeare Library of Washington, D.C., from whose holdings the vast majority of the pictures reproduced here are taken, as will be seen in the Notes on Illustrations section at the end of the book. So to the Trustees, to the Director, Dr. Louis B. Wright, and to the Curator of Books and Manuscripts, Dr. Giles E. Dawson, who extended permission, go my special thanks. While I was Research Professor on the staff of the Folger, I enjoyed thumbing through the Library's holdings of English books published prior to 1640, and during the course of this endeavor I selected many of the pictures reproduced here. Photographs of these illustrations were taken by Mr. Horace Groves, the Folger's photographic expert, whose unsurpassed skill and unfailing good spirits I shall never cease to appreciate. The earliest form of this illustrated life was presented as a lecture in 1964 at the Cosmos Club in Washington, to mark the four-hundredth anniversary year of Shakespeare's birth, and the response of my fellow members there encouraged me to expand this earlier form into the present volume. At various points along the way, I have greatly profited from the criticisms and suggestions of Giles E. Dawson and James G. McManaway, my former colleagues on the staff of the Folger Shakespeare Library, and of Gerald Eades Bentley of Princeton University. To each of these friends and associates I extend hearty thanks for what they have contributed to this book.

Permission to publish a photograph of the Globe model (Fig. 59) by J. C. Adams and Irwin Smith was kindly supplied by Mr. Adams.

The drawing of *Titus Andronicus* on the stage (Fig. 35) is reproduced by the kind permission of the Marquess of Bath.

The small portrait-print of Henry Carey (Fig. 36) is reproduced through the courtesy of the British Museum, which holds the original.

The Cambridge University Press kindly consented to my reproducing the engraved portrait of the Elector Palatine and his bride (Fig. 104).

The Richard Burbage portrait (Fig. 60) is reproduced from the original in the Dulwich College Picture Gallery, with the cooperation of the Governors.

Photographs of the Memorial Bust of Shakespeare were taken by Holte Photographics, Ltd., and appear here (Figs 2-3) with permission of Holy Trinity Church, Stratford-upon-Avon.

J. Q. Adams' theatrical map of London and his reproduction of a detail from Agas' map of London (Figs. 33 and 17) appeared in Adams' *Shakespearean Playhouses* (1917) and appear here through the courtesy of the publisher, the Houghton Mifflin Company.

The illustration from Brathwait's *Ar't Asleepe Husband?* (Fig. 113) is reproduced by permission of The Huntington Library, San Marino, California.

The University of Liverpool Press allowed me to reproduce the sketch of Gower (Fig. 65) from their *Pericles*.

The picture of the tavern owned by Thomas Quiney (Fig. 110) is reproduced by permission of Methuen and Co., Ltd.

The Chandos Portrait and the portrait of King Henry VIII (Figs. 4 and 106) may be found in the collections of the National Portrait Gallery, London, and are reproduced from photographs kindly supplied by that gallery.

The print of Ratsey (Fig. 81) is reproduced here through the courtesy of Professor T. J. B. Spencer on behalf of the Shakespeare Association.

The picture of St. Helen's Church, Bishopsgate (Fig. 40) is reproduced by permission of the rector.

Scott, Foresman and Company extended permission to reproduce the "Pipes and Ale" drawing (Fig. 103) which appeared in their publication of Hardin Craig's edition of the *Complete Works of William Shakespeare* (1951).

Doctors John Kapp Clark and Adrian Buyse, formerly of Smith, Kline, and French Laboratories, helped me to find the picture (Fig. 86) of an early apothecary's shop, and Mr. W. B. McDaniel II, Curator of Historical Collections of the Library of the College of Physicians of Philadelphia, kindly permitted me to reproduce the illustration from a volume in that Library's collections.

The Yale University Library courteously allowed the Meriden Gravure Company to reproduce certain pictures from their collections for use in this book (Figs. 15, 46, 72, 101).

In each instance, the source of the figures reproduced in the text is given in the Notes on Illustrations list at the end of this book, but I wish to underscore my thanks at this point, in addition to the bibliographical acknowledgments given there.

I wish also to express my appreciation to the Meriden Gravure Company, which has so skillfully reproduced the illustrations for this book, and especially to John Peckham, who has shown so much interest in the work.

Thanks of a special kind go to Princeton University Press, with which it is always a pleasure to work: to its director, Herbert S. Bailey, Jr., who has been in every way helpful with this book; to P. J. Conkwright, in whose hands book-making becomes art; and to my editor, Polly Hanford, who has not only made suggestions that have improved this book at point after point, but who has done so with such charm and sweetness that her corrections have not only been recognized and appreciated, but even enjoyed.

Then there is my wife Jean, who has an unfailing ear for the proper rhythms of English prose as well as for the problems and enthusiasms of an author-husband, and who can still never be thanked enough for everything.

Portraits of Shakespeare

1. Shakespeare's Bust in Stratford

THE story of a great man's life tells us much about him, but we also wish to know, if we can, what he looked like, so that we may visualize him as we read his biography. Fortunately, we have two authenticated likenesses of Shakespeare, of which the earliest is the memorial bust in his native parish church in Stratford-upon-Avon. The second portrait is the engraving on the title page of the first collected edition of the plays, which was published seven years after his death and which is reproduced elsewhere in this book. (See frontispiece and Fig. 114.) In that edition of the plays, Leonard Digges wrote a poem "To the Memory of the Deceased Author Master William Shakespeare" in which he referred both to Shakespeare's works and to the sculptured portrait over the tomb in Stratford:

> *Shakespeare, at length thy pious fellows give*
> *The world thy Works: thy Works, by which,*
> * outlive*
> *Thy Tomb thy name must: when that stone*
> * is rent,*
> *And Time dissolves thy Stratford monument,*
> *Here we alive shall view thee still. This book,*
> *When brass and marble fade, shall make thee*
> * look*
> *Fresh to all ages.*

We know, then, that the monument was completed no later than seven years after Shakespeare's death.

2. Shakespeare's Bust, Another View

THE Shakespeare monument was executed in Gloucestershire limestone by Gheerart Janssen (anglicized as Gerard Johnson), an Anglo-Flemish tomb-maker whose shop in Southwark was within a block or two of the Globe Theatre, so that he had presumably seen Shakespeare in the flesh many times. We have no comment as to how closely the figure represents Shakespeare's appearance, but Shakespeare's wife and children were sufficiently satisfied with it to have had it installed in the church. After the fashion of those times, it was placed on the wall of the church, while the grave itself was under the floor.

The monument was originally painted to represent Shakespeare's complexion, but with the passing years the original paint was chipped or worn down, and in the eighteenth century the monument was entirely repainted in "good stone color," to fit the classical tastes of that century. The present colors date only from a repainting of 1861, and are of little or no value.

There is a description of Shakespeare by one of his friends in the London theatrical world, Christopher Beeston, who told his son that Shakespeare "was a handsome, well-shaped man: very good company, and of a very ready and pleasant smooth wit."

3. The Memorial Inscription

THERE are two inscriptions on Shakespeare's monument, one written in English and the other in Latin. Like the comment of Digges, both inscriptions refer us beyond Shakespeare's effigy to his writings. The English inscription declares of Shakespeare's fame and worth as a writer that his

> name doth deck this tomb
> Far more than cost: see, all that he hath writ
> Leaves living art but page to serve his wit.

And the Latin inscription describes him in terms of the great figures of classical literature:

> A Nestor in judgment, a Socrates in genius,
>   a Virgil in art:
> The earth covers him, the people mourn him,
>   and Olympus has him.

As the monument was erected by Shakespeare's family, the Latin inscription is most likely the work of his son-in-law, Dr. John Hall.

4. The Chandos Portrait

THE Stratford monument and the Folio engraving of 1623 certainly represent Shakespeare. Many other portraits have been claimed as likenesses, but of these the Chandos portrait shown here has the best credentials. Once owned by the Duke of Chandos, from whom it takes its name, its ownership may be traced through Thomas Betterton, the Restoration actor and authority on Shakespeare's life, to Sir William Davenant, who was Shakespeare's godson. Davenant, Betterton, and Dryden all evidently regarded the portrait as a painting of Shakespeare, and it may be that they were right, though it is by no means certain.

Stratford-Upon-Avon

5. The Pleasant Town of Stratford-upon-Avon

STRATFORD was the place of Shakespeare's burial, as it was of his birth, and since his own time it has been closely associated with him in the popular mind. Less than a dozen years after the publication of Digges's poem on Shakespeare's works and his Stratford monument, it was apparent that the monument was a tourist attraction. In the late summer of 1634, a Lieutenant Hammond wrote of Stratford that "in the church in that town" there was "a neat monument of that famous English poet, Mr. William Shakespeare, who was born here," while in 1630 an earlier writer described Stratford as "a town most remarkable for the birth of famous William Shakespeare." Close personal friends and associates of Shakespeare seem to have thought of him almost instinctively in relation to Stratford-upon-Avon. Ben Jonson thus referred to him as "sweet swan of Avon," while John Lowin, who acted in many of his plays and was his business associate in the Globe Theatre, applied the same words to him. Sir William Davenant, who from his earliest childhood had known Shakespeare, wrote that at his death each flower on the banks of the Avon hung its head in mourning, while the river wept itself dry, to show its loss. Shakespeare's own close and lasting attachment to his native town will become clear as the story of his life unfolds.

6. A Church of England Baptism

SHAKESPEARE's birth date is not recorded in Stratford, but his baptismal date is, for in the sixteenth century the date of baptism was considered far more important than the date of birth. The parish register of Holy Trinity Church, Stratford-upon-Avon, notes that on April 26, 1564, William Shakespeare was christened in the church, and since christening usually took place within a few days after the birth, the birthday has been generally assumed to be April 23. Though merely an arbitrary choice, this date does provide a nice symmetry to Shakespeare's life, for he died on this same date, fifty-two years later, April 23, 1616.

Shakespeare was the first son and third child in a family of eight children born to John Shakespeare (d. 1601) and his wife Mary Arden Shakespeare (d. 1608). John Shakespeare's family were yeomen, while Mary Arden's people were an ancient family of landed gentry, and Mary's father had been landlord to John's father. The marriage of yeomen into the gentry was not uncommon in sixteenth-century England, especially when the yeoman involved was so obviously a rising man as was the young John Shakespeare.

7. Shakespeare's Boyhood Home

SHAKESPEARE'S parents owned this house at the time of his birth, and he was presumably born here. During this period Stratford was a prosperous country village of some 1,500 inhabitants, living in 200 or more houses. Such a town would compare to London in Shakespeare's day as an American city of 100,000 would compare to Washington and New York today.

The town records show John Shakespeare's increasing prominence in Stratford affairs, as he was elected to the most important offices, including that of mayor. Some people today love to draw a picture of Shakespeare's father as an il-literate, but the Stratford records do not support this charge. It is true that the elder Shakespeare seems persistently to have signed his name with a mark, but this was a common practice followed by many Elizabethans who could write perfectly well. If we wish to know whether John Shakespeare was literate, we had best look elsewhere for more conclusive evidence, and this we have in the fact that he was not only elected but re-elected town chamberlain, with responsibility for keeping all the records and accounts. Had he been illiterate, the town council might just conceivably have made the mistake of electing him chamberlain or secretary-treasurer once (though even this is unlikely), but it is quite inconceivable that they would have reelected him.

Scale, one Inch and a half to a Foot.

8. Religious Art Defaced by Shakespeare's Father

WHILE John Shakespeare was acting as chamberlain, it was decided by the town corporation of which he was a member that the wall paintings in the Guild Chapel should be plastered over, as they smacked too much of "popery" for the protestant Church of England. Exercising his official responsibility for supervision of town property, John carried out the task thoroughly, and reported that the medieval paintings were no longer visible as of January 10, 1564. The picture here shows what was left of the saints' images (telling the story of Saint Helena and the true cross) after John Shakespeare's plaster was removed in the nineteenth century.

In 1565 John was also charged with the responsibility of seeing to the repair of the schoolmaster's house, and at a somewhat later time with selecting a new schoolmaster for Stratford. In 1568 he was elected bailiff or mayor of Stratford, a position of much prestige and one which automatically entitled him to a coat of arms had he wished to pursue his application, which at this time he did not do. As bailiff, he paid four shillings to a group of strolling actors for performing in Stratford. At the time, William Shakespeare was five years old. If he saw the play, it was presumably his first contact with the stage, but during the following years there were a number of such performances in Stratford.

9. A Merchant Displays his Wares

STRATFORD was a market town for its region in Warwickshire, and as such enjoyed considerable prosperity. As a tradesman, John Shakespeare would lay out his wares in much the same fashion as is shown in this picture, using his house and the street in front of it. Referred to by his fellow townsmen as a glover and leather-dresser, and as a dealer in wool and farm produce, John seems to have been a typical small-town entrepreneur. He enjoyed an apparently growing prosperity for a number of years, but from 1577 until his death in 1601 his fortunes went into a decline from which he was rescued only by the success of his dramatist son.

William Shakespeare was at the impressionable age of fourteen when his father's financial difficulties became apparent in the records. In 1578 the father paid no poor tax, a clear sign of trouble, and the evidence increased as the years passed. He ceased to attend meetings of the Stratford Council, of which he had been so diligent a member; he mortgaged some property, and sold part of his wife's share in her inherited estate; he was cited to come before the court of Queen's Bench to provide surety that he would keep the peace, and when he failed to appear was very heavily fined. By 1587 he was replaced as alderman because he would not come to meetings and had not come for a long time. His absenteeism extended to church, and in September 1592 he was listed for failure to attend church—a legal fault in an age when church attendance was required by statute. It has sometimes been claimed that the elder Shakespeare stayed away from Church of England services because he was a Roman Catholic, or because he was a Puritan, but the evidence is against such claims. The official records state that John Shakespeare was absent "for fear of prosecution for debt." We cannot know definitely the root cause of his difficulties, but the story reminds us of the classic decline of the alcoholic.

10. Stratford's School and its Chapel

THE Stratford Guild Chapel is shown on the corner of the street in this picture. It was here that John Shakespeare plastered over the medieval paintings of saints, and it was here that William Shakespeare would have attended worship services every day as a Stratford schoolboy. The Stratford Grammar School was located in the half-timbered houses just beyond the chapel, and beyond the school are the quarters provided by the town for its poor. The school was located a few blocks from Shakespeare's boyhood home on Henley Street, and there may be a note of personal reminiscence in the lines Shakespeare later wrote about

the whining school-boy, with his satchel
And shining morning face, creeping like snail
Unwillingly to school.

Shakespeare probably entered this school at the age of six or seven.

11. Elizabethan Schoolboys Reciting in Class

IN Elizabethan grammar schools the grammar studied was Latin, not English. Before entering a grammar school a boy had already learned to read and write English, and was prepared to go on to a rigorous training in Latin, with a great deal of systematic drill not only in Latin grammar but also in logic, rhetoric, composition, versifying, and public speaking—all in Latin. Boys of all ages studied together and recited in the same room, under a Latin master, as shown in this Elizabethan print. The teachers at Stratford-upon-Avon in Shakespeare's school days were exceptionally well prepared, all holding both bachelor's and master's degrees from Oxford University, and they were attracted by a salary equal to that paid at Eton and other leading schools. The Stratford school in Shakespeare's youth was as good as any school in England, and far better than most. Here Shakespeare would come to know quite well such classical writers as Terence, Cicero, Virgil, Horace, Juvenal, Martial, Seneca, and the Ovid who remained such an obvious favorite during his own active career as a writer. Authorities on the history of education agree that Shakespeare was well prepared by this Stratford curriculum to go on to his own creative work in later years. There is also an ancient tradition, better founded than most such traditions, that before he moved to London and his theatrical career he had himself worked as "a schoolmaster in the country."

12. A Water Pageant for Queen Elizabeth

In Elizabethan England schoolboys did not give over their entire time to study any more than boys do today. There were many other interesting things to do. In 1575, for example, the Earl of Leicester staged a spectacular water-pageant for the entertainment of Queen Elizabeth at his great Kenilworth estate. Kenilworth was only a dozen miles northeast of Stratford, and as people from miles around came to see the entertainment, it may well be that the eleven-year-old Shakespeare was present at this spectacle. Shakespeare the dramatist later referred in two of his plays to such a pageant—once in *Midsummer Night's Dream* (2.1.155-65) and again in *Twelfth Night* (1.2.15), where the reference is specifically to "Arion on a dolphin's back," one of the striking features of the Kenilworth production.

The picture shown here is of a similar entertainment arranged for Elizabeth in 1591 at Elvetham by the Earl of Hertford.

13. Anne Hathaway's Home

THIS is the house of Richard Hathaway, a well-to-do farmer of Shottery, a village about a mile from Stratford. On September 1, 1581, Richard Hathaway made his will, and in it he indicated that his daughter Anne was already engaged and that her marriage was expected soon. In Elizabethan times marriages were legally recognized when they were entered into by the vows of bride and groom with the consent of their parents, usually taken before witnesses of family and friends. It was often only at a later time that the marriage was solemnized in the church. Ecclesiastical law, dating well back into the Middle Ages, forbade the solemnizing of marriages during certain prohibited seasons of the year (Advent and Lent), so that in 1582 it was virtually impossible for a couple to be married between December 2, 1582, and April 7, 1583.

14. Bishop Whitgift and a Special Marriage License

A FEW DAYS before the beginning of this prohibited season, a marriage license was sought to authorize William Shakespeare and Anne Hathaway (c. 1556-1623) to be married in church without the required proclamation of the banns—or announcement of the intent to marry by the preacher from the pulpit on three successive Sundays or holy days.

This appeal was made on November 28, 1582, to the episcopal church court at Worcester, the diocese of Bishop John Whitgift. Whitgift was later Archbishop of Canterbury (1583-1604). His lifelong record and his reputation for the strictest adherence to church law assure us that the marriage was approved only on the soundest basis of conformity to Anglican church law. The groom was eighteen at the time, and the bride twenty-six.

15. Marriage—and a Family

ABOUT six months later, on May 26, 1583, William and Anne Shakespeare's first child was baptized in Holy Trinity Church, Stratford. It was a daughter, and she was named Susanna (1583-1649).

Two years later, twins were born to the couple, and baptized on February 2, 1585, as Judith (1585-1662) and Hamnet (1585-1596). This unusual combination of names for a boy and girl seems to indicate that the twins were named after Judith and Hamnet Sadler, who were presumably the godparents. Hamnet Sadler was a Stratford baker, and a lifelong friend of Shakespeare. These were the only children. The two girls grew up and married, but Hamnet, Shakespeare's only son, died at the age of eleven.

Early Years in the Theatre

16. Varieties of Renaissance Entertainment

AFTER the baptism of the twins in 1585, we lose contact with Shakespeare for several years. The next contemporary reference to his location comes seven years later, in 1592, and shows him by that time to have become quite well established in the theatrical profession.

But to use "profession" in connection with the Elizabethan theatre is to invite the wrong impression. Elizabethans did not think of the theatre as a profession, but lumped actors with bearbaiters, bullbaiters, and acrobats, and placed them all only a little if at all above the level of rogues and vagabonds. The picture shown here combines in a single view the major varieties of the entertainment business of Shakespeare's time and country, though it is in fact set in Venice rather than London. In the left foreground two acrobats are doing tumbling stunts, while in the center of the picture are actors performing on an outdoor stage. To the left of the actors, dogs are baiting a bear, while in the top part of the picture a bull is fighting back at the mastiffs attacking it.

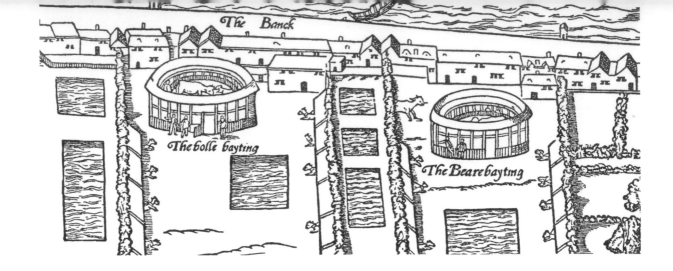

17. Bull- and Bearbaiting Rings

ONE of the favorite entertainments for Elizabethan Englishmen was to visit the bull- and bearbaiting rings just across the Thames river south of the City of London. It would be hard to imagine a bloodier sport, with the dogs snarling and snapping at the bulls till they were bloody all over, and the bulls goring and tossing the dogs on their horns or trampling them with their hooves. Sometimes the dogs would "wearie" a bull or a bear till he was dead at the stake to which he was tied, but the casualties among the dogs were so great that in 1592 about 120 had to be kept in kennels like those shown here so that a sufficient number would be available to provide the action which the public loved. An advertising bill of the time announced also a humorous interlude "for your better content" of the "pleasant sport" of whipping the blind bear Harry Hunks "till the blood run down his old shoulders." Such were the popular entertainments of the time, and the theatres were in daily competition with these bloody sports. It is small wonder that the stage plays tended so much to violent action.

18. The Popularity of Executions

WITNESSING public executions was another popular pastime among Shakespeare's contemporaries, who were fascinated by the shedding not only of animal but also of human blood, a fact which we need to remember if we are to understand the violence of Elizabethan stage tragedies. Many of the same people who went to the theatre also attended public executions to see the blood spurt as the headsman's axe severed head

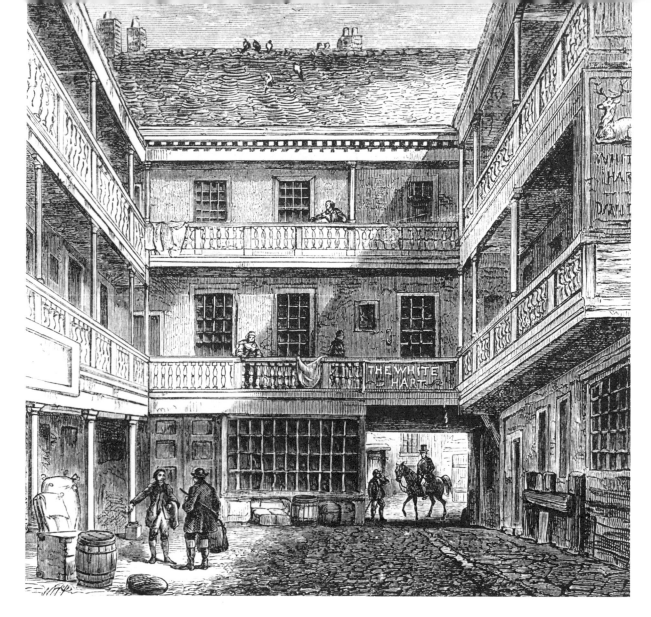

from shoulders on the block, or as the executioner cut down a half-strangled victim hanging from the gallows in order to disembowel and dismember the still-living corpse.

19. The White Hart: An Innyard for Players

IT WAS in such a society that Elizabethan drama developed, and this of course includes Shakespearean drama. We do not know when Shakespeare began either to write for the stage or to act on it—or what he was doing between the baptism of his twin children in 1585 and his emergence as an established actor-dramatist in 1592. These are the only years for which we do not have solid evidence of the activities of the mature Shakespeare, and they are therefore known as "the lost years."

Deductive conclusions are quite possible, however, and we know that Shakespeare must have been in London long enough before 1592 to have learned his trade thoroughly, and to have completed his theatrical apprenticeship. This would seem to suggest that he became involved with theatrical activities not too long after 1585. Certainly, some of his early theatrical experience would have been with courtyards of inns such as the one pictured here, where the actors would set up their stage at one end and play to an audience collected in the yard and on the balconies. The permanent theatre buildings erected around Elizabethan London after 1576 preserved much of the feeling of these innyards, by their placing of stage, yard, and galleries.

20. Richard Tarlton, the Popular Clown

IF Shakespeare had anything to do with the London theatrical world by 1588, he either knew personally or at least knew of Richard Tarlton, who died in September of that year. Tarlton was one of the most popular performers of his time, both with the general public and with the Queen herself. "A joyous jester and buffoon," he also tried his hand at playwriting, but he was best known and most influential as a comic actor. He set the style for the clowns, and was closely followed in comic technique by Shakespeare's colleague, Will Kempe, of whom we shall see more a bit later (see Fig. 61). It was in such a mold that Shakespeare created the clowns of his first decade of writing.

21. *The Spanish Tragedy* by Thomas Kyd

IF Tarlton established the acting pattern for raucous comedy, Thomas Kyd (1558-1594) in his play *The Spanish Tragedy* set the tone for writ-

22. *Doctor Faustus,* by Christopher Marlowe

ing Elizabethan tragic drama. Written about 1589, this play appears to have created the revenge tragedy as a literary form. Illustrated here is the father's discovery of the murder of his son, which he must revenge. In *Hamlet*, this early revenge pattern was reversed so that the son would avenge the father's murder, but many of the key elements found in Kyd's tragic formula were retained: a ghost calling for revenge, feigned madness, and a play within the play. With its exciting interaction of plots and counterplots, and its compounding of assassination with assassination, *The Spanish Tragedy* may not be great literature, but it was thundering good theatre, and one of the most influential plays in the history of the drama.

WRITTEN at about the same time as *The Spanish Tragedy*, Christopher Marlowe's *Doctor Faustus* is a far more sophisticated drama. Excitement the play certainly provided, with its conjuring up of devils on the stage (as shown here), and the later carrying away of Faustus to hell, but it also had a poetic power which marks it as an enduring literary masterpiece. Marlowe (1564-1593), with his "mighty line," demonstrated how blank verse could be used to produce both good theatre and great poetry. Marlowe's scandalous character and career set him apart from the respectable, "honest," and gentlemanly qualities which contemporaries remarked on in Shakespeare, but his poetry undoubtedly influenced Shakespeare's early writings.

23. Edward Alleyn, the Famous Tragedian

THE leading roles both in *The Spanish Tragedy* and in *Doctor Faustus* were taken by Edward Alleyn (1566-1626), the most famous actor at the time. Only two years younger than Shakespeare, Alleyn resembled his great contemporary in that he made a considerable fortune in the theatre (greater, indeed, than Shakespeare's seems to have been), and retired to live the life of a country gentleman. His financial success may be traced to two facts: he was a very capable actor, and in 1592 he married the daughter of Philip Henslowe, one of the great theatrical magnates of the time. After his retirement, Alleyn bought the manor of Dulwich in 1605, and endowed a school there called the College of God's Gift at Dulwich, which he provided not only with money but with many invaluable theatrical records. (The school continues to this day, and is one of the better English public schools.) The improved social status of the theatre is indicated by the fact that after the death of his first wife, Alleyn in 1623 married the daughter of John Donne, famous poet, Dean of St. Paul's, and friend of King James. To be sure, Donne felt even then that his daughter had married beneath herself, but thirty years earlier such a marriage would not have taken place at all.

24. *Friar Bacon and Friar Bungay*, by Robert Greene

IT IS the early period which concerns us now, for a bitter attack on Alleyn in 1590 can tell us something about a similar reaction to Shakespeare. The attack came from Robert Greene (1558–1592), one of the principal writers for the London stage in its formative years between 1587 and 1592. One of Greene's most popular plays, a very amusing comedy called *Friar Bacon and Friar Bungay*, is represented here by an illustrative print from its title page.

Greene was university educated, and his contempt for Alleyn and most of his theatrical associates was a mixture of social and educational snobbery with a heavy salting of economic envy. Writings plays—even highly successful plays such as Greene's—was not very lucrative, whereas acting and theatrical ownership could be extremely profitable. Greene bitterly resented this fact, and so he attacked Alleyn as a "crow" (that is, a stupid bird who had been taught to say a few words he could not understand) who was "prankt with the glory of others' feathers" (that is, one who won glory by acting out the words which his "betters" had written). It was a vicious comment, but only a dress rehearsal for what Greene would have to say about Shakespeare.

25. A Cutpurse

GREENE was a dissolute fellow who lived a hand-to-mouth existence among the pickpockets, cut-purses, bawds, and whores of London's criminal quarters. He was a kind of Elizabethan beatnik, who supported himself by writing lurid confessions of his own and other people's sins. He hated success and respectability, especially in anyone whose initial advantages had been less than his own. In 1592, he discharged his animus against the young Shakespeare.

Like Alleyn, Shakespeare was "an upstart crow, beautified with our feathers," Greene warned the university-trained writers of London. But Shakespeare was a far worse threat than the actor Alleyn, for Shakespeare even presumed to write plays as well as to act in them, and, as Greene put it, "with his *Tiger's heart wrapt in a player's hide*, supposes he is as well able to bombast out a blank verse as the best of you: and being an absolute *Johannes factotum*, is in his own conceit the only Shake-scene in a country." With the close paraphrase of a popular line from Shakespeare's *3 Henry VI*, and the allusion to Shake-scene, Greene made himself unmistakably clear. By 1592, Shakespeare was established as a successful actor-dramatist, and Greene hated him for his success.

26. A Gentleman

THOUGH Greene died soon after writing his attack, it was published at his dying request by his literary executor, Henry Chettle (c. 1560-c. 1607). Shakespeare never dignified it with a public reply, but his friends protested, and a meeting took place between Shakespeare and Chettle. Thereafter, Chettle acted the part of a gentleman and issued a printed apology. He had not known Shakespeare when he saw Greene's pamphlet through the press, Chettle declared, but had since met him and now very much regretted that he had ever allowed the offensive passage to be published. "I am as sorry," Chettle wrote, "as if the original fault had been my fault, because myself have seen his demeanor no less civil than he excellent in the quality he professes. Besides, divers of worship have reported his uprightness of dealing, which argues his honesty, and his facetious grace in writing, that approves his art."

With Chettle's apology, the unpleasant incident was closed. It shows us that the twenty-eight-year-old Shakespeare was not only well established but also highly regarded by men of standing ("divers of worship"), if not by a Bohemian like Greene. And we hear him described in terms which others also would later apply to him: that he was honest in his dealings, and civil or gentlemanly in behavior.

27. Thomas Nashe

THOMAS NASHE (1567-1601), shown here in an Elizabethan cartoon, was a Cambridge graduate and a popular writer of the late 1580s and the 1590s, who began like his friend Robert Greene to attack the players and playwrights of London but came later to admire and defend them. In a work published in the fall of 1592 he praised Edward Alleyn as the equal of the greatest actors of the classical world, and also gave clear evidence of the stage popularity of one of Shakespeare's plays. "Ten thousand spectators at least (at several times)," Nashe declared, saw on the stage "brave Talbot (the terror of the French)," who was one of the principal characters in the first part of Shakespeare's *Henry VI*.

From Greene, Chettle, and Nashe, then, it is clear that by the fall of 1592 Shakespeare was well established as an actor and a successful dramatist in London.

The Plague Years
and the Narrative Poems

28. The Plague Diverts a Rising Career

AT the very time that we get these early evidences of Shakespeare's growing reputation, a severe attack of the bubonic plague was building up in London. The plague, or black death, was the great scourge of Europe and could sweep away 10 percent of the population within a few months. It is difficult for us, with our efficient modern programs of public health and preventive medicine, to imagine the terror that came with the plague.

This print, from a book of Shakespeare's age, gives the death figures for two continental cities and shows how at the height of an epidemic

in Basile 1633
died. 20000

in Trent. 1634
died. 30000

bodies were simply thrown out into the streets. The same practice was followed in England.

Theatrical people feared the plague even more than others did, for even if it did not end their lives it would certainly put an end to their public performances and so to their means of livelihood. When deaths from the plague exceeded thirty or forty a week in London, the theatres were all ordered closed to prevent the spread of the disease through large congregations of people. Between June 1592 and May 1594 the theatres were closed most of the time, or for a total of almost two years. During this period the old theatrical companies and alignments were radically disrupted.

29. Death Cart and Gravedigger at Work

THE plague, building up throughout the summer of 1592, became epidemic by August. It continued through 1593, when 11,000 died in London alone, and carts such as that shown here went through the streets to the cry of "Bring out your dead." The bodies, loaded on the carts, were then taken out to be buried en masse.

30. *Venus and Adonis*

IT was during this period of theatrical inactivity that Shakespeare's two long poems appeared. *Venus and Adonis* was entered for publication in April 1593, and *Lucrece* in May 1594.

These two beautiful narrative poems, though certainly not Shakespeare's greatest works, are the only works which he carefully proofread and saw through the press. This fact is highly significant. Though we regard these poems as being among Shakespeare's good, but minor, productions, he himself devoted to their proper printing a care which he never expended on any of his plays. Indeed, none of the eighteen plays by Shakespeare which were printed during his lifetime shows any evidence of his having taken an interest in its accurate publication. He appears to have held the opinion of many of his contemporaries that plays were not a very important literary form, and if he agreed at all with those among his contemporaries who regarded him as a very great literary genius, he has left us with no evidence of that fact, and perhaps with much evidence against it. But his two long poems he regarded differently, for poetry as such was thought of as art, and a proper occupation for a gentleman.

Formosam sequitur flagrans Dea Cypria Adonim, In̄q̄ sinu inuenies requiem modo ducere gaude
Et nunc̄imbelles sollicitare feras.   Osculaque in roseis figere longa genis.

31. *Lucrece*

WITH *Lucrece*, Shakespeare established himself among his contemporaries as a morally serious poet, just as he had evidenced his abilities as an amatory poet the year before with his *Venus and Adonis*. The earlier of the two poems was regarded as sexually inflammatory, as several Elizabethan references indicate, and Shakespeare appears to have been intent upon showing another, more philosophical side of his talent when he came to write *Lucrece*. As the first poem focuses upon the lustful passion of the goddess of love, so the second focuses upon the moral reflections of the chaste Roman wife Lucrece, who was raped by Tarquin and who committed suicide to escape her shame. *Venus and Adonis* was written in the lighter sesta rima stanza form, and the evidence from Shakespeare's younger contemporary Sir John Suckling (1609-1642), along with other contemporary evidence, indicates that Shakespeare at first wrote sections of *Lucrece* in the same form, but then changed to the more "serious" rhyme royal stanza. Five stanzas are preserved in the earlier six-line form, and we can see that Shakespeare usually converted these to the final seven-line form by merely inserting an additional line, thus avoiding any lengthy rewriting. This speedy method of composition bears out what Shakespeare's friends John Heminges, Henry Condell, and Ben Jonson all tell us—that Shakespeare wrote fast, and that he did not devote much time to "blotting" or revision.

32. Shakespeare's Early Patron, the Earl of Southampton

HENRY WRIOTHESLEY (1573-1624), 3d Earl of Southampton, was Shakespeare's patron during 1593 and 1594, the plague years when the two long poems were published, as we know from the fact that both poems were dedicated to him. The first dedication implies only a slight acquaintance, and although the second shows more assurance, neither indicates any great degree of intimacy when judged by Elizabethan customs and standards. To assume that Shakespeare was an intimate friend of one of the great lords of his time is to act apart from evidence, and indeed against what we know of Elizabethan social mores.

Venus and Adonis and *Lucrece* were alone among the more than seventy issues and editions of his works (including eighteen plays) published in his lifetime, in that for them only did Shakespeare write dedications, just as it was only for them that he engaged in careful proofreading before they were issued to the public in print. The reward which a patron such as Southampton would have given him for the two dedicated works probably helped Shakespeare weather the bad times when the theatres were closed, and may later have helped him to buy a share in a newly formed acting company, the Lord Chamberlain's Men. After 1594, there is no evidence of any personal association between Shakespeare and Southampton.

Later Years
in the London Theatrical World

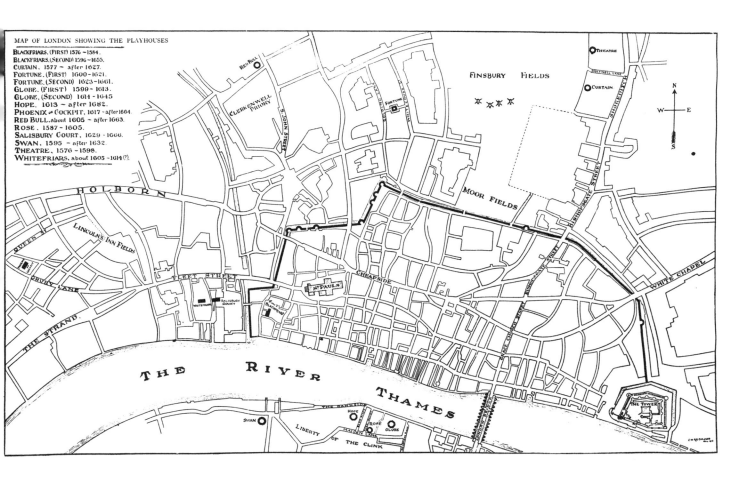

MAP OF LONDON SHOWING THE PLAYHOUSES
BLACKFRIARS, (FIRST) 1576 – 1584.
BLACKFRIARS,(SECOND) 1596 – 1655.
CURTAIN, 1577 – after 1627.
FORTUNE, (FIRST) 1600 – 1621.
FORTUNE, (SECOND) 1623 – 1661.
GLOBE, (FIRST) 1599 – 1613.
GLOBE, (SECOND) 1614 – 1645.
HOPE, 1613 – after 1682.
PHOENIX or COCKPIT, 1617 – after 1664.
RED BULL, about 1605 – after 1663.
ROSE, 1587 – 1605.
SALISBURY COURT, 1629 – 1666.
SWAN, 1595 – after 1632.
THEATRE, 1576 – 1598.
WHITEFRIARS, about 1605 – 1614 (?).

33. Map of London Playhouses

THESE poems represent only an episode in Shakespeare's writing career. When the theatres were allowed to reopen in May 1594, after the abatement of the plague, we find Shakespeare in his own element again as a playwright and actor.

This map shows the location of the various London theatres in Shakespeare's time. At one time or another, Shakespeare himself acted or his plays were performed at the Rose and New-ington Butts, but his most continuous associations were with the following theatres in London: The Theatre in the warmer months and the Cross Keys Inn during the winter months from 1594 till at least the spring of 1597; the Swan for at least part of the time during 1596-1597; the Curtain from 1597 to 1599; the Globe exclusively from the spring of 1599 until his company took over the Blackfriars theatre in August 1608, and thereafter both the Globe and the Blackfriars until his retirement from the stage.

34. *Titus Andronicus:* Shakespeare's First Printed Play

Titus Andronicus was the first of Shakespeare's plays to be printed. As shown here, the title page of that first edition did not carry the author's name, as publishers at that time rarely acknowledged the authors of the plays they printed. Furthermore, most theatre-goers did not know who wrote even the most popular plays. Even today, few movie-goers or television-viewers can name the authors of their favorite shows, and the author's name is headlined only when it

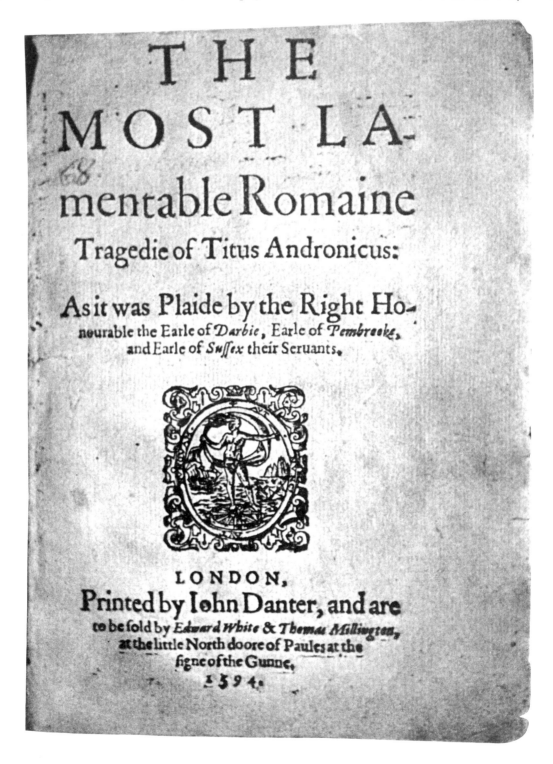

will attract an audience. The same was true to an even greater extent in Shakespeare's day; and although Shakespeare was already well known in theatrical circles it was not until 1598 that he was so well known among the general public that publishers found his name would sell their printed books. When that time came, his name not only appeared on his own plays but was placed by unscrupulous printers on works with which he had no connection.

35. *Titus Andronicus* on the Elizabethan Stage

THE staging of *Titus Andronicus* in an early performance is illustrated in this drawing, made about 1594. We can see here that Elizabethan productions made no consistent effort at historically accurate costuming: there was an unmistakable attempt to make Titus look like a Roman general, which he is in the play, but the other characters were anachronistically dressed in Elizabethan clothes. Aaron the Moor, the villain of this play, is also interesting, for he was made up in intense black-face, giving us an indication that Shakespeare's other Moor, Othello, was also presented on the stage as a black man.

Titus was Shakespeare's first tragedy. A bloody and violent play, it is dramatically effective, but it shows signs of being the apprentice work which in fact it was. It is a horror play of the first order, which is what we should expect from a young dramatist of Elizabethan times. The remarkable fact is not that Shakespeare began his tragic career by writing a coarse melodrama, but that he so soon progressed to the highest stage of tragic poetry. Ben Jonson indicated that the play dated from about 1589 or even earlier. Our first possible reference to it on the stage comes in 1592, and soon after the plague had abated and the theatres reopened, we know that it was performed at Newington Butts in June of 1594 by the newly formed acting company called the Lord Chamberlain's Men.

36. Henry Carey, The Lord Chamberlain

THE Lord Chamberlain's Company was formed in 1594 after the devastating plague, and was established under the patronage of Henry Carey (c. 1524-1596), the first Lord Hunsdon, who was a favorite cousin of Queen Elizabeth, and her Lord Chamberlain. After Henry Carey's death, his son George Carey, the second Lord Hunsdon who also became Lord Chamberlain at a later date, assumed the patronage. It was a remarkable company in many ways. Though the company, following contemporary practice, took its name from its patron, it was actually owned and operated by some eight professional theatrical people. Of these, along with others whom we shall see later, William Shakespeare was one.

Beginning in 1594, Shakespeare's associations with this company continued throughout the most important years of his theatrical career, and indeed for the remainder of his life. At the accession of King James to the throne in 1603, the company was taken under his patronage and assumed the name The King's Men, but under whatever name, it was the most successful theatrical company of its time and perhaps the most significant in the history of the drama.

37. Queen Elizabeth

QUEEN ELIZABETH (1533-1603) enjoyed the drama, though, as a frugal Tudor, she never devoted as much money to it as did her successor, James I. We know from Ben Jonson's explicit

testimony that Shakespeare was a favorite dramatist of Elizabeth's, just as he was later a favorite of King James. Furthermore, during the last decade of Elizabeth's reign the Chamberlain's Men was by far the most popular company at court, putting on thirty-two known performances before the queen as compared with thirty-three known performances by all the rival companies combined.

The popular modern legends of close friendship between Shakespeare and Queen Elizabeth are, historically speaking, preposterous. Ben Jonson makes it clear that it was Shakespeare's dramatic "flights" that "so did take Eliza." The Virgin Queen (and her virginity was attested by medical examination) was a very great ruler, not the least of whose achievements was providing conditions which encouraged the development of great drama. She and her Stuart successors to the throne protected theatrical people from the antagonism of London officials, who would not allow theatres to operate freely in the city of London proper. It was for this reason that the theatres were constructed outside the mayor's jurisdiction, either beyond the walls to the north, or over the river to the south, or in ancient "liberties" within the city which were exempt from city control.

39. A Rowdy Evening in Gray's Inn Hall

MANY of the most sophisticated and intelligent people in London during Shakespeare's time belonged to the so-called Inns of Court, which were a combination of law schools, professional societies, and gentlemen's clubs. At certain times of the year, the Inns of Court either put on plays of their own or employed the regular dramatic companies to act before them. On such an occasion, December 28, 1594, Shakespeare's *Comedy of Errors* was performed on a temporary stage erected at the end of this hall at Gray's Inn before what was described at the time as "a disordered tumult and crowd." The Gray's Inn party had evidently gotten out of hand early in the evening and some of the honored guests were offended and left, but the players were of course in no position to leave. The play did not begin until well after 9:00 P.M., and though the tumult subsided somewhat there was still enough "to disorder and confound any good intentions whatsoever," as the contemporary description put it. This supposedly fashionable audience at Gray's Inn was rowdier by far than any we know of at the Globe in Shakespeare's lifetime.

38. Performances at Greenwich Palace

DURING the Christmas festivities of 1594, on December 26 and 27, the Chamberlain's Men performed two plays before Elizabeth and the royal court at Greenwich Palace, shown here. Court records show that £20 was paid directly to Shakespeare and two of his fellow owners of the company, Will Kempe and Richard Burbage, for these two performances. Playing at court was profitable for Shakespeare and his company, but as there were on the average only about three such "command performances" a year, their major source of support had to be the general public rather than the crown. It was in the public theatre, indeed, that Shakespeare's genius grew, as he learned to appeal to all sorts and conditions of men.

40. Shakespeare's Parish: St. Helen's, Bishopsgate

PRIOR to 1596, and during the first part of that year, we know that Shakespeare lived within the parish of St. Helen's Church, Bishopsgate, shown here. This put him about half way between the location of The Theatre north of Bishopsgate on the City Wall and the Cross Keys Inn in the central part of the city, the two principal stages for his company at this time.

The size of the tax assessment which Shakespeare paid in this parish on February 1, 1596, may indicate that he had his family with him, for the assessment would be quite high for a single man and would indicate a house large enough for a family. But in November 1597 the tax collectors noted that they could not find Shakespeare at his old address, and the same report was entered until 1599 when it was noted that he then lived in Sussex. The delinquent taxes were transferred to the proper jurisdiction south of the river Thames and were paid there by Shakespeare. This change of residence would have put Shakespeare closer to the new center of operations for his company, on Bankside, where the Globe Theatre would be erected in a few years.

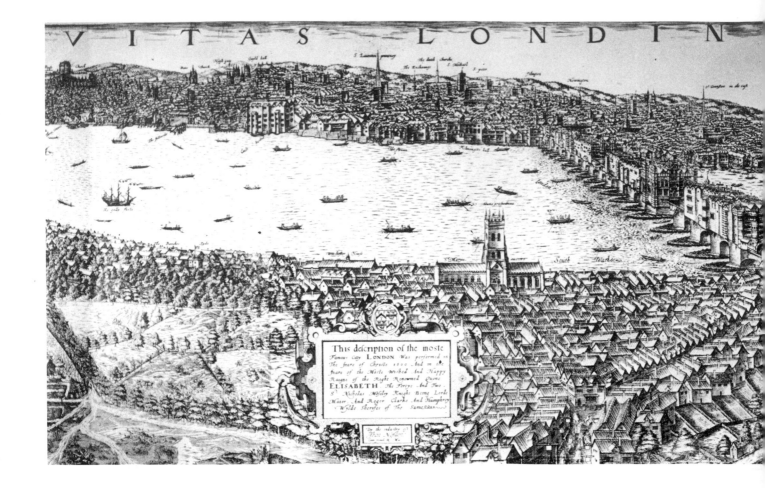

41. A New Neighborhood: Southwark and Bankside

SOMETIME after Shakespeare moved south of the river and took up his residence in Southwark, in the neighborhood shown in the left-hand side of this picture-map, a very interesting incident occurred. On November 29, 1596, a certain William Wayte swore in court that he feared for his life from William Shakespeare, Francis Langley (owner and builder of the new Swan Theatre in Southwark), and two others. This action seems to have come in retaliation against a similar court action taken by Langley, alleging that he was threatened by the same William Wayte and his stepfather, an unsavory and unscrupulous local justice of the peace named William Gardiner. Gardiner and Wayte are thought by some to be the originals on which Shakespeare patterned Justice Shallow and his nephew Slender in *The Merry Wives of Windsor.*

This Gardiner was surely an untrustworthy character, but we do not know the nature of the unpleasantness between his faction and Shakespeare. The evidence does, however, show Shakespeare living on Bankside and associated with the owner of the new Swan Theatre there (see Fig. 42). It also provides another interesting insight into Shakespeare's character. Shakespeare was evidently not associated with tavern brawling as was Marlowe, or with killing his duelling opponents as was Ben Jonson, or with the criminal element of London whom Greene fancied. Indeed, he was "gentle" Shakespeare, but "gentle" meant gentlemanly, and gentlemen carried swords, and the Wayte case shows that Shakespeare could be a difficult man to deal with when he was aroused.

42. The Swan Theatre

THE Swan Theatre in Southwark is shown here in a sketch of its appearance in 1596, when Shakespeare was associated with it and with its owner. According to an account written at that time, the Swan was London's finest theatre; it would accommodate 3,000 spectators, and had wooden columns so skillfully painted to resemble marble that even an acute observer might be deceived.

The action on the stage may be of one of Shakespeare's plays, as the Lord Chamberlain's men were playing here at about this time, but there is no way of knowing this, and the picture has much more important things to tell us about typical Elizabethan stage conditions. As in the old inns, there were three tiers of galleries in which the spectators might sit if they paid an additional fee. Otherwise they stood as groundlings in the pit or yard surrounding the stage on three sides. The groundlings, who paid the minimum admission fee, were exposed to sun and rain, since the "wooden O" was without a roof in the center. Spectators in the galleries could sit on benches and were protected from the elements by the roof. A roof also extended over a portion of the apron stage; called by various names—the "heavens," or shadow, or cover—this roof provided the actors with some protection against rain and sun, and it also housed machinery for raising and lowering stage properties. The flag flying from the roof would indicate to Londoners that a play was scheduled or in progress, and the trumpeter in the upper right furnished another form of advertising.

*Shakespear ye Player
by Garter*

43. Shakespeare's Coat of Arms

ON October 20, 1596, the Shakespeares were granted this coat of arms, and were henceforth recognized as members of the English gentry. The arms were officially granted because of "faithful and valiant service" rendered to King Henry VII by an unnamed ancestor, and because the family had continued to be "of good reputation and credit," but a more important reason was probably Shakespeare's own growing stature and repute. Henceforth he could, and did, sign himself as "William Shakespeare, gentleman." In a class-conscious society, this was an important and gratifying honor. It was an honor to which the Shakespeares evidently felt themselves entitled, for they chose as their family motto the phrase *Non sanz droict* (not without right). The Grant of Arms also declared that this recognition was for the encouragement of the Shakespeare posterity.

Shakespeare must have seen in that phrase a certain sad irony, for two months previously, on August 11, 1596, his only son and male heir, Hamnet, had been buried at Holy Trinity Church in Stratford. The boy was only eleven years old at the time of his death. With him died Shakespeare's hope of establishing a line of Shakespeares as a permanent part of the gentry of Warwickshire.

44. Shakespeare's Stratford Home: New Place

FOR Shakespeare, the major event of the following year, 1597, was his purchase on May 4 of one of the finest houses in Stratford-upon-Avon. The house was known as New Place, and is shown here in a later picture based on a survey made in 1599, within two years of Shakespeare's purchase but after he had been able to complete certain work on the place which he seems to have undertaken soon after it came into his hands. He paid £60 for the house, a handsome sum at the time, but in return he got a handsome house. This was the first major nontheatrical investment that Shakespeare made, to our knowledge, and it was followed by a number of shrewd investments over the next several years as Shakespeare built up an estate out of his earnings in the theatre.

45. Ben Jonson

THOUGH Shakespeare's family seat was established at New Place in Stratford-upon-Avon, his career interests continued to be in London. One of his best-known associates there was Ben Jonson (1572-1637), whom he met at least as early as 1598. Brilliant, learned, and arrogant, Ben Jonson was the exception to almost every rule of English society and drama in his time. Never one to be unsure of himself, Jonson spoke on many subjects, and from him we learn a good deal about Shakespeare: that he was "gentil"; that he was not only proof against malice, but above the ill fortune of having to contend with it; that the actors often praised him, and resented criticism of him; that he was a favorite dramatist both of Queen Elizabeth and King James; and finally a brief, eloquent tribute to his character: "He was indeed honest, and of an open, free nature."

Jonson's view of Shakespeare as a writer was also high. For him, Shakespeare was "Soul of the age! / The applause, delight, and wonder of our stage," but he was also much more, for "He was not of an age, but for all time." In tragedy he rivaled the greatest classical dramatists, and exceeded them all in comedy. Indeed, as Jonson said, "I lov'd the man, and do honor his memory (on this side idolatry) as much as any." Surely none of Shakespeare's contemporaries accorded him higher praise than did Ben Jonson.

46. The Question of Shakespeare's Learning

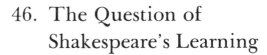

JONSON'S admiration of Shakespeare was not unmixed, however, and we shall see a number of examples of his criticism. The most famous, biographically, is the charge that Shakespeare had "small Latin, and less Greek." This comment provides insight into both men. Both had enjoyed excellent opportunities at fine "secondary" schools, but neither had attended a university. Both continued their own educations by private reading, but Jonson pursued his studies so avidly that he became recognized as one of the most learned men of his time, a reputation which he wholeheartedly enjoyed. There was at least a trace of pedantry about him (he could even footnote one of his own plays), but his scholarship was genuine and he was awarded an honorary degree by Oxford University. This was the background for Jonson's disparagement of Shakespeare's learning, and for the charge that Shakespeare "wanted art." By Jonson's own standards, the charges may be true, but they are misleading. Another contemporary, an anonymous but prolific editor whose scholarship fell far short of Jonson's, even referred to Shakespeare as "a learned writer."

47. Hales of Eton Defends Shakespeare

As FOR Shakespeare's learning, the truth lies somewhere between these two remarks, as Jonson himself was willing to admit in his long poem on Shakespeare. We can find similar testimony elsewhere. Thus the widely educated Leonard Digges took account of Jonson's charge by saying in effect that if Shakespeare had "wanted art," he nonetheless showed "art without art unparalleled as yet," far preferable to Jonson's "tedious (though well labored)" tragedies. And Robert Burton, whose learning equaled Jonson's, called Shakespeare "an elegant poet."

Finally, there is an old story (which may be apocryphal, but sounds fairly authentic), of a literary gathering at which Jonson was criticizing Shakespeare for his "want of learning and ignorance of the ancients," and John Hales (1584-1656), the long-time fellow of Eton College and one of the most respected scholars of his time, replied that if Shakespeare had not studied the ancients, he had likewise not copied them as Jonson did, and that if Jonson "would produce any one topic finely treated by any of them, he would undertake to show something upon the same subject at least as well written by Shakespeare." To the substance of that remark, "rare Ben" Jonson would probably have agreed, as we can see from his own high praise of his friend's work.

48. Francis Meres Recognizes Greatness

IT WAS NOT to Ben Jonson, however, that credit must go for the first recognition of Shakespeare's greatness. The first man who publicly appraised Shakespeare at something like the stature accorded him by succeeding generations was a Cambridge graduate and country parson named Francis Meres (1565-1647). In a work published late in 1598 and entitled *Palladis Tamia: Wits Treasury*, Meres wrote the appraisal of Shakespeare which appears here in a reproduction of the original text. Significantly, Meres compared Shakespeare to Ovid for his poetry and for his plays to Plautus and Seneca, the great Latin masters of comic and tragic drama.

In the same year, a country gentleman, minor poet, and Oxford man named Richard Barnfield (1574-1627), classified Shakespeare with Spenser, Daniel, and Drayton among the best regarded poets of his own time and country, and declared that Shakespeare's name would live forever "in Fame's immortal book." These remarks show that Shakespeare was beginning to overcome the social prejudice against theatrical work which was widely felt by the people of his time. And though Meres and Barnfield were doubtless still in a minority in their very high regard for Shakespeare, there is other evidence that his fame was steadily growing.

As the foule of *Euphorbus* was thought to liue in *Pythagoras* : fo the fweete wittie foule of *Ouid* liues in mellifluous & honytongued *Shakefpeare*, witnes his *Venus* and *Adonis*, his *Lucrece*, his fugred Sonnets among his priuate friends, &c.

As *Plautus* and *Seneca* are accounted the beft for Comedy and Tragedy among the Latines : fo *Shakefpeare* among ÿ Englifh is the moft excellent in both kinds for the ftage; for Comedy, witnes his *Gētlemē of Verona*, his *Errors*, his *Loue labors loft*, his *Loue labours wonne*, his *Midfummers night dreame*, & his *Merchant of Venice*: for Tragedy his *Richard the 2. Richard the 3. Henry the 4. King Iohn, Titus Andronicus* and his *Romeo* and *Iuliet*.

As *Epius Stolo* faid, that the Mufes would fpeake with *Plautus* tongue, if they would fpeak Latin : fo I fay that the Mufes would fpeake with *Shakefpeares* fine filed phrafe, if they would fpeake Englifh

A

PLEASANT

Conceited Comedie
CALLED,

Loues labors loſt.

As it vvas preſented before her Highnes
this laſt Chriſtmas.

Newly correĉted and augmented
By *W. Shakeſpere.*

Imprinted at London by *W.W.*
for *Cutbert Burby.*
1598.

49. *Love's Labour's Lost,* with Shakespeare's Name

IN THE same year in which the comments of Meres and Barnfield appeared, publishers found that sales were helped by putting Shakespeare's name on his books, and *Love's Labour's Lost* was the first of his published plays to be credited to him on the title page. This came four years after the publication of his *Titus Andronicus* in 1594 (see Fig. 34). In omitting Shakespeare's name from his plays, publishers were merely reflecting the general Elizabethan disregard for contemporary drama as literature, and they treated other important dramatists such as Thomas Kyd and Christopher Marlowe no better. As there was no author's copyright law until the eighteenth century, the author had no recourse once a publisher had obtained his book (whether fairly or not) and had entered his possession in the official Stationers' Company Register.

50. Bookshop

SHAKESPEARE's plays which found their way into print in his lifetime were sold in bookshops somewhat like this one. The picture shows how books were displayed for sale by placing them flat against shelves, like magazines in modern drug stores. The titles are crudely indicated in this sketch by the rectangles on the exposed title pages. The books were put on display without bindings. If a purchaser wanted a book bound, he would have to arrange for a binder to do the work, as the bookseller displayed his wares in paper covers.

The sale of his plays did not bring Shakespeare much income, if any, for Elizabethan authors had no rights in their printed works, which were legally vested in the publishers. Furthermore, if a publisher bought a play manuscript for publication, the purchase money would rarely if ever go to the author. For a "pirated" play, the publisher would pay the person who illicitly sold the manuscript. In a legitimate purchase the money would go to the theatrical company to which the author had already sold his play, and not to the author himself who no longer owned it. This was the standard system of Shakespeare's time, and for him to have promoted the publication and sale of his dramatic manuscripts would have seemed dishonest. The company would as a rule try to keep the plays out of print until their drawing power at the box office had begun to wane, but might then sell a copy to a publisher. Any money realized from the sale of one of Shakespeare's plays to a printer would normally have gone into the gross income of the company, to be shared by all the stockholders.

51. A Shakespeare Folio and Quarto

THE smaller of the two volumes pictured here is a quarto. It was in volumes of this size that eighteen of Shakespeare's plays appeared during his lifetime, one play per quarto. When Shakespeare died in 1616, half of his plays were still unprinted, but seven years after his death his long-time theatrical associates and friends John Heminges and Henry Condell collected thirty-six Shakespearean plays and had them published in a single volume, the First Folio of 1623, which is the larger of the two volumes in this picture.

Some of the quartos present fairly good texts, honestly obtained and printed. Other quartos, however, were "stolen and surreptitious copies, maimed and deformed by the frauds and stealths of injurious impostors," as Heminges and Condell wrote in the First Folio. It is important to note here that even the most carefully printed quartos contain errors so obvious that no author could conceivably have missed correcting them had he ever read proof on the printed texts. Analysis by Gerald E. Bentley of one of the best quartos suggests that it contains one hundred times more errors per thousand lines than are to be found in the two long poems which Shake-

speare carefully supervised in the press. Shake-speare obviously took no interest in the print-ing of his plays and for reasons we have already considered this would have seemed to his associ-ates a natural and proper attitude for him to take. His responsibility was for his plays on the stage, not in print.

52. Going to Press

HERE, in a typical English printing shop of Shakespeare's time, we see printers operating their press. Even more important for our inter-ests, however, is the man working at the slanted case on the right. He is the compositor or type-setter, setting a page in type by taking letters out of the type case before him as he reads the copy to be reproduced in print. He is obviously the key man in transforming the play manuscripts into the printed versions through which we now know Shakespeare's works. Since Shakespeare did not proof or otherwise supervise the print-ing of his plays, the accuracy of the texts de-pended largely on the compositors who set them in type. Much research has gone into studying the techniques of the men who set type for Shakespeare's plays, and we now know a great deal both about their general methods and about the kinds of errors to which particular ones were prone, so that it is possible to correct many of these errors and solve many problems regarding Shakespeare's original wording and intent.

53. Shakespeare as a Theatrical Writer

THERE were over three hundred other writers in Shakespeare's age who also contributed plays to various theatres. Shakespeare was obviously the greatest genius among these writers, but he also had another advantage over them, and this was his unrivaled technical mastery of every aspect of the theatre. No man before or since has for so many years been so intimately involved with every facet of the drama—acting, writing, managing, and owning—as was Shakespeare. From his writings it is obvious that he was a genius, but it is equally obvious to anyone who knows the subject that he had a professional mastery of every phase of theatrical operation.

Three of Shakespeare's friends tell us that he wrote with great facility, scarcely blotting a line, and it is clear that he must have worked fast to have accomplished all that he did. He also must have worked hard and one of his theatrical associates, Christopher Beeston, told his son, William Beeston, that Shakespeare was "the more to be admired that he was not a company keeper . . . wouldn't be debauched."

54. Thomas Heywood on Playwrights, Printers, and Shakespeare

DURING his own period, Shakespeare's name was often associated with that of Thomas Heywood (1573-1641). Heywood was chief dramatist for Queen Anne's Company—one of the rivals to Shakespeare's group—and was also an actor. He expressed the general conviction of the profession that honesty prohibited making "a double sale of their labors, first to the stage, and after to the press," a statement which applies equally to Shakespeare's apparent attitude toward publication. Heywood also informs us of one of Shakespeare's brushes with the publishing world.

Beginning in 1599, the London publisher W. Jaggard had issued several editions of a book called *The Passionate Pilgrim*, a collection of poems ascribed to Shakespeare, though only a minority of the poems are his, and in 1612 he published a "newly corrected and augmented" edition which contained some of Heywood's verses, still under Shakespeare's name. Heywood protested Jaggard's action, and said of Shakespeare that "I know [him] much offended with Mr. Jaggard that, altogether unknown to him, presumed to make so bold with his name." But, since the existing laws protected publishers' rather than authors' copyright, there was little the two men could do about such injustices. Heywood also protested against the undue familiarity with which people called poets by nicknames, and cited the treatment of Shakespeare:

Mellifluous Shakespeare, whose enchanting quill
Commanded mirth or passion, was but Will.

55. The Globe Theatre

IN 1599, Shakespeare's involvement in the theatre became even more extensive than it had been before, for he and his associates in the Lord Chamberlain's Men had decided that they would no longer rent a theatrical building, but would build their own theatre, to house the acting company they owned and operated. The new theatre, called the Globe, is shown here in an early map. It was built just south of the Thames River, on Bankside in Southwark. An inventory dated May 16, 1599, refers to the Globe as "newly built" at that time, and "in the occupancy of William Shakespeare and others." This was the first time that actors had owned the theatre in which they performed. It was a landmark in theatrical history, and also in Shakespeare's life.

56. Actors on the Apron Stage

CERTAIN differences between the early and modern stages must be clearly understood if we are to understand Shakespearean drama in its own terms, and the most important of the differences concerns intimacy of effect. The stage for which Shakespeare wrote was not placed off in a box behind a picture frame, and separated from the audience by footlights and orchestra pit. The Elizabethan public stage jutted right out into the audience, which surrounded it on three sides. Within such a setting, the aside and the soliloquy seem perfectly natural. Furthermore, there was little or no heavy scenery to be moved about, and so a far greater speed of dramatic action and a far more sustained emotional concentration could be achieved.

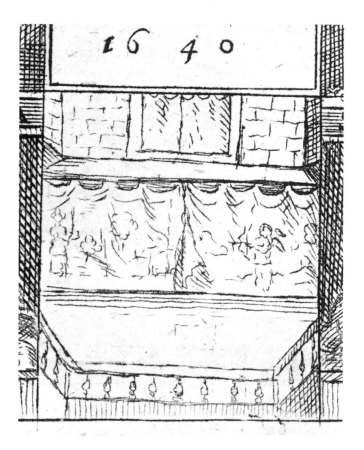

57. Bare Apron Stage

THIS continuity of effect was one of the great advantages of the English Renaissance stage. Action followed action, event followed event, without break in the sustained development. As elaborate stage settings were absent, no time was lost in changing scenery. There were no intermissions in the performance at public theatres such as the Globe, no dropping of the curtain to indicate the end of scenes and acts. This was not a drama of places and scenery, but of poetry, events, and personalities. Nothing distracted the audience from the massive cumulative development of style, action, and characterization.

those particular performers. And he carefully calculated the number of individual parts in a play, along with the number of characters who would be onstage at any time in the play, so that the play could be efficiently performed by the personnel of his company at a given time. Thus there are about forty speaking parts in *Julius Caesar*, but these are so deployed that the play can be convincingly acted by about fifteen persons. And we know that this was the size of the Lord Chamberlain's company when, according to the eye-witness account of Thomas Platter, the play was "excellently performed" at 2:00 P.M. on the afternoon of September 21, 1599.

59. The Globe Theatre, Interior

A RECONSTRUCTION of the Globe Theatre is shown in this model by John C. Adams and Irwin Smith, which is now in the Exhibition Gallery of the Folger Shakespeare Library.

The size of the stage was approximately 43 by 27 feet, and the audience in the pit stood on three sides around this stage, while those who had purchased more expensive places were seated on benches in the three levels of the galleries, which again surrounded the stage in a horseshoe arrangement. In this way, the persons seated farthest from the stage were about as close as a person sitting in the twelfth row of a typical modern theatre with a picture-frame stage. Furthermore, the design of English Renaissance theatres allowed for much larger audiences than most modern theatres afford. Two independent estimates, made in London at the time, agree in setting the audience capacity at 3,000.

And the audience at the Globe was clearly a cross section of London society. This was not a class theatre, whether upper or lower; nor was it a coterie theatre, appealing only to a self-appointed group of sophisticates. It was indeed a theatre for everyman.

58. The Globe Theatre, Exterior

IT WAS for this Globe Theatre that Shakespeare's greatest tragedies were written. The succession including *Julius Caesar*, *Hamlet*, *Othello*, *King Lear*, *Macbeth*, and *Antony and Cleopatra* was originally envisioned for this stage in the years between 1599 and 1607.

The plays were not only constructed for this stage but for the particular actors of Shakespeare's own company. When Shakespeare wrote a play, he knew just who would perform the major roles and just what he could expect from

60. Richard Burbage, Shakespeare's Great Tragic Actor

RICHARD BURBAGE (c. 1568-1619), shown here, was certainly one of the greatest actors of his time, and probably the greatest. He and Shakespeare were not only partners in the ownership and operation of the Chamberlain's Men—the Elizabethan term was "sharers" or "fellows"—but evidently remained close friends till the end, for when Shakespeare died in 1616 Burbage was one of his "fellows" to whom he left a gift of money for the purchase of a memorial ring.

We know from contemporary references that Burbage acted the roles of Richard III, Hamlet, Lear, and Othello, as well as many others. In addition to his acting, Burbage was a well-known amateur painter, and may have painted the original portrait of Shakespeare from which the Droeshout engraving for the first folio was copied. Like most of the "sharers" of the Chamberlain's, he appears to have been a thoroughly reputable citizen. He was married, had at least eight children, and lived near his brother Cuthbert on Halliwell Street in the Shoreditch section of London. Like Shakespeare, he accumulated a comfortable fortune from the theatre.

We have a lively description, published in 1604, of Burbage's performance as Hamlet. According to Anthony Scoloker, Hamlet tore at his clothes until he was clad only in his shirt, started and stared, ran about and suddenly stopped still, snapped his fingers, and acted the part as a raving lunatic. It is a vivid description of a very vigorous performance, but Scoloker unfortunately did not say whether Hamlet was merely feigning this madness or whether he was supposed to be really mad. He did, however, comment that the play had the power to "please all," and he referred to the author as "friendly Shakespeare," thus providing another glimpse into the poet's personality.

61. Will Kempe, the Clown who Danced Away

ON the right is Will Kempe, one of the great clowns of the Elizabethan stage. This picture shows him as he made a famous hundred-mile trip from London to Norwich, doing a Morris dance all the way, in the late winter of 1600. By this time he seems to have left the Lord Chamberlain's Men, of which he had been one of the founding sharers in 1594, and to have sold his share in the Globe Theatre. But for at least six years before this time he had played principal comic roles in Shakespeare's plays. Prompter's notes printed in the texts of the plays show that he acted the role of Peter in *Romeo and Juliet* and of Dogberry in *Much Ado About Nothing*. His forte was broad comedy, farcical bumbling, and fairly obvious physical clowning. To fit Kempe's style of acting, Shakespeare created such parts as Costard in *Love's Labour's Lost*, Launce in *The Two Gentlemen of Verona*, and Bottom in *A Midsummer Night's Dream*.

62. Robert Armin, and a New Comic Style

ROBERT ARMIN (d. 1615), shown in this print, succeeded Kempe as the principal clown with Shakespeare and his fellows at the Globe. Armin's comic style differed markedly from that of Kempe, and though he could also act such roles as Dogberry, he was a more subtle comic. Where Kempe was especially adept at dancing and cavorting, Armin was a skillful singer, given to a more bitter-sweet humor.

Accordingly, Shakespeare created a different kind of clown to suit Armin, and the older more extroversive clowning disappears from the plays written after this change of acting personnel.

Characters such as Feste in *Twelfth Night*, the First Gravedigger in *Hamlet*, and the Fool in *Lear* were created for Armin. This shift does not indicate that Shakespeare's outlook on life was somehow disrupted and soured at about this time. It merely indicates that he knew how to make the most of the particular acting skills available to him under any given circumstances. In this shift of comic styles we see at once the versatility of Shakespeare's genius and the practicality of his approach.

63. John Lowin, and his Shakespearean Roles

IN 1603 this actor joined Shakespeare and his fellows at the Globe. His name was John Lowin (1576-1669?), and he began as a hired man, though he was an experienced actor, and he

64. Falstaff and the Hostess

seems to have become a sharer in the company no earlier than 1604. We know from the first folio that he played in Shakespeare's plays, and we know from Ben Jonson's testimony that Lowin and Shakespeare both acted in Jonson's tragedy *Sejanus* in 1603. Tradition has it that Lowin also played the parts of Shakespeare's Henry VIII (he appears to have been built for the role) and Falstaff. In later years, he became one of the directors of Shakespeare's company.

THIS picture of Falstaff and the Hostess dates from a period some thirty or thirty-five years after Shakespeare's death, but while John Lowin was still alive. There is enough similarity between this Falstaff and Fig. 63 to indicate that we may have here a sketch of Lowin as Falstaff. Perhaps not, and the point isn't an important one, but this is an interesting early drawing of Falstaff, and a very pleasant one.

Iohn Gower.

65. Gower, the Chorus to
Pericles

THIS picture may give us some further insight into the stage costumes used in Shakespeare's plays. The drawing represents John Gower, the medieval poet, and an attempt seems to have been made to provide him with at least a modified version of medieval dress. Gower was chorus to *Pericles*, a play which Shakespeare wrote in collaboration with others, probably late in 1607 or early in 1608. Presumably be- cause it was a collaboration, Heminges and Condell did not include the play in the 1623 folio.

It was a popular play, nonetheless, especially with London's diplomatic community. A con- temporary Venetian said of it that "All the am- bassadors who have come to England have gone to the play more or less," and that the Venetian Ambassador Giustinian took the French Am- bassador and his wife and the Secretary of Florence to *Pericles*, in a theatre party which cost him "more than 20 crowns."

66. Shakespeare on Shipboard

WITH all the professionalism displayed in them, however, Shakespeare's plays were still not the exclusive province of professional actors. They also attracted amateur actors, even sailors on a long sea voyage. At about the same time that *Pericles* was attracting the diplomatic corps to the London theatre, Captain William Keeling of the East India Company Ship *Dragon* off Sierra Leone had his crew perform *Hamlet* on shipboard (September 5, 1607, and March 31, 1608) and also *Richard II* (September 30, 1607) for the entertainment of visitors aboard his ship and also "to keep my people from idleness and unlawful games, or sleep." Even this early it seemed natural for Englishmen to take a copy of Shakespeare with them wherever they might go in the course of building an empire.

67. Caliban?

ONE of the most striking of Shakespeare's characters is Caliban, in *The Tempest*. He was conceived and presented as a "fish-like" monster, "a strange fish," with fin-like arms who yet looked strangely like a man. How could such a character have been presented in the theatre? We have, to be sure, no authentic picture of Caliban on Shakespeare's stage, but it is possible to make an educated guess, using Elizabethan books which picture exotic and mythical animals. Shakespeare and his contemporaries were fascinated with descriptions by explorers and others of far-away, outlandish, and even nonexistent creatures. One such creature is shown here in a

picture which was published several times during Shakespeare's life; the picture gives some hint as to how an actor might have been made up to play the part of Caliban on Shakespeare's stage.

68. Shakespeare in Kingly Roles?

BUT what roles did Shakespeare himself play? A late tradition says that he played the ghost in *Hamlet*, and an even later one that he played old men's roles, but neither story is very authoritative. Quite probably, he was not a great actor, for though he was frequently referred to by his contemporaries as an actor, as well as a dramatist, his contemporaries usually did not identify the characters he portrayed. There was one possible exception, when the dramatist George Peele has the Scottish king in his historical play *Edward I* (c. 1592–1593) told to accept the overlordship of the title character, King Edward of England:

Shake thy spears in honor of his name,
Under whose royalty thou wearest the same.

Granting the Elizabethan love of punning, Peele may here have been playing with the actor's name (Shake-spear) who played the role of the king, but the identification is by no means certain. At all events, John Davies of Hereford (c. 1565–1618), the Oxford instructor in writing, says Shakespeare did play the part of kings. At the same time he compares Shakespeare to the great Latin dramatist Terence, and further reinforces the impression of Shakespeare as genial, witty, and honest:

To our English Terence, Mr. Will. Shake-
speare
Some say (good Will) which I, in sport, do
sing,
Hadst thou not played some Kingly parts
in sport,
Thou hadst been a companion for a King,
And been a King among the meaner sort.
Some others rail; but rail as they think fit,
Thou hadst no railing, but a reigning wit:
And honesty thou sow'st, which they do
reap;
So to increase their stock which they do
keep.

Jonson in 1623. These references cumulatively link Shakespeare with writing plays, acting in plays, and living in Stratford.

It was characteristic of the Elizabethans that they not only thought of themselves in terms of their classic predecessors, but also that they thought of their predecessors in terms of themselves. Thus the picture shown here—which is a representation of the theatre of Terence in a Renaissance edition of his plays—is in reality so close to the Elizabethan theatre and so far from the Roman theatre that it may have been merely an adaptation of what Londoners knew from their own experience as playgoers.

69. "Our English Terence" and his Theatre

SHAKESPEARE's early comedies show considerable influence from the Latin comedies of Plautus (c. 254–184 B.C.) and Terence (c. 185–159 B.C.) a fact which is to be explained both by his own solid grounding in the Latin classics and by the strong formative influence of Latin drama upon Elizabethan drama as a whole. Not only was Shakespeare influenced by these comic playwrights, but he was also explicitly compared to them as his reputation grew. As we have just seen, he was hailed by Davies as "our English Terence," and similar comparisons were made by Francis Meres in 1598, by the anonymous writer of the preface to *Troilus and Cressida* in 1609, by Thomas Freeman in 1614, and by Ben

70. An Historian Asks for More

HAVING surveyed the conditions of Shakespeare's stage and the acting resources available to him, let us now return to his life where we left it at the time of the completion of the Globe Theatre in 1599. In that same year, the gentleman pictured here, a Cambridge-trained antiquary or historian named John Weever (1576-1632), wrote a poem in honor of Shakespeare, in which he explicitly compared Shakespeare as a poet and dramatist to Apollo, the god of art. He particularly commended Romeo, Richard, Venus and Adonis, and Tarquin and Lucretia as "thy children, Shakespeare," and called on him to "beget" many more. At about the same time or a little later the well-known litterateur Gabriel Harvey (c. 1545–c. 1630), who had been both a Cambridge student and teacher, noted that "the younger sort takes much delight in Shakespeare's *Venus and Adonis*, but his *Lucrece* and his tragedy of *Hamlet, Prince of Denmark* have it in them to please the wiser sort."

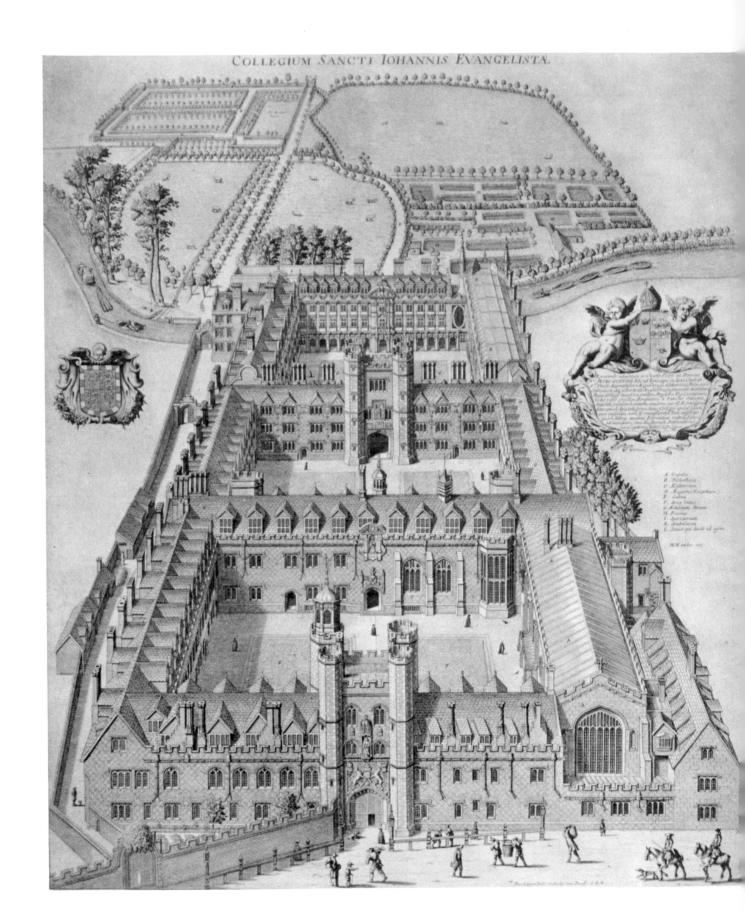

COLLEGIUM SANCTI IOHANNIS EVANGELISTÆ.

71. Cambridge Students Discuss Shakespeare

SHOWN here is St. John's College, Cambridge, which was the scene of three plays, probably enacted during the Christmas seasons of 1598, 1599, and 1601, and now called the Parnassus Trilogy. These plays are rather typical of those written and put on by university students at the time, but they have a particular interest for what they say about Shakespeare. One student, a character in the plays, declared that Shakespeare was a better poet than Chaucer or Spenser, and said that he wanted Shakespeare's picture to hang in his room. In another of these plays we are told that Shakespeare had a better wit than any of the learned writers of the time, including Ben Jonson. There is even the tantalizing statement that "Shakespeare hath given him [i.e., Ben Jonson] a purge that made him bewray his credit." We do not know the incident alluded to here, but there are other traditions of Shakespeare's having put Jonson in his place.

72. Thomas Fuller on Shakespeare's Repartee

THE most delightful story about Jonson and Shakespeare comes from Thomas Fuller (1608-1661), one of the most famous historians in the seventeenth century. Writing as an historian, Fuller provides the obvious information about Shakespeare's birth and burial in Stratford, and also gives a brief character sketch of Shakespeare, saying that "his genius generally was jocular, and inclining him to festivity, yet he could (when so disposed) be solemn and serious, as appears by his tragedies." He then writes this lively description of the wit-combats:

"Many were the wit-combats betwixt him and Ben Jonson, which two I behold like a Spanish Great Galleon and an English Man of War: Master Jonson (like the former) was built far higher in learning; solid, but slow in his performances. Shakespeare, with the English Man of War, lesser in bulk but lighter in sailing, could turn with all tides, tack about and take advantage of all winds, by the quickness of his wit and invention."

means, Essex on February 8, 1601, tried to raise a rebellion in the streets of London. The intended uprising was a dismal failure. Essex was captured, and, within three weeks, executed.

This was the only known occasion on which Shakespeare's writings got his company in trouble with the law. On the day before the uprising, Essex supporters paid the Chamberlain's Men to stage Shakespeare's *Richard II* at the Globe, since that play concerned "the deposing and killing" of a king, and thus might be effective propaganda for their rebellion against Elizabeth. The play did not materially aid their cause, but a careful official investigation was made into the company's part in the whole business. The testimony showed that they were quite unaware of Essex's plot, and they were exonerated. Indeed, they played before Elizabeth at Whitehall Palace on the eve of Essex's execution.

73. The Earl of Essex: A Favorite turned Traitor

ROBERT DEVEREUX (1566-1601), 2nd Earl of Essex, was one of Elizabeth's great favorites, and one of the few instances in which she badly misjudged character. Vain and dangerously ambitious, he had achieved some military distinction when in 1599 the chorus in Shakespeare's *Henry V* called him "the general of our gracious empress," and expected him to crush the Tyrone rebellion in Ireland. Instead, Essex adopted a policy of appeasement with Tyrone, and was disgraced with Elizabeth. Desperate, and shut off from further advancement by legitimate

74. A Successful Performance in Middle Temple Hall

ABOUT a year after the Essex affair, Shakespeare's comedy *Twelfth Night* was performed as the principal feature at a great feast in the Middle Temple on February 2, 1602. Another one of the great Inns of Court, the Middle Temple provided Shakespeare with a more civilized audience than he had found at Gray's Inn when *The Comedy of Errors* was performed there some eight years earlier. The stage was set up at one end of the great hall shown here, and the play was well received, the character of Malvolio having been commented on as especially amusing.

A few weeks later, other amusing comments were going the rounds at the Middle Temple, this time about Shakespeare himself.

75. A Scandalous Story, or the Story of a Scandal?

ACTORS have always attracted the attentions of ladies in the audience, and amusing stories, usually scandalous, have always attached themselves to well-known names, especially theatrical or political names. As a general rule, it is wise not to take such stories too seriously as biographical evidence. Even at the time, it is difficult to determine their accuracy, and after three and a half centuries it is impossible. Students especially love to tell these tales, and on March 13, 1602, a law student in the Middle Temple named John Manningham recorded the following story as having been told him by one of his fellows there:

"Upon a time when Burbage played Richard III, there was a citizen grew so far in liking with him that before she went from the play she appointed him to come that night unto her by the name of Richard the Third. Shakespeare, overhearing their conclusion, went before, was entertained, and at his game ere Burbage came. Then message being brought that Richard the Third was at the door, Shakespeare caused return to be made that William the Conqueror was before Richard the Third. (Shakespeare's name William.)"

NON APTVS EST REGNO DEI

76. Farming the Land

EVEN while he was most actively following his dramatic activities in London, Shakespeare maintained a continuing interest in his native village of Stratford and the country surrounding it. He seems to have had a deep affection for the land and the people who lived close to it. Time and again, as his personal fortune grew, he invested it in one or another form of farming property near Stratford.

Thus on May 1, 1602, just a few months after his performance at the Middle Temple, he bought over one hundred acres of farm land from his Stratford friends William and John Combe, paying £320 for the lot. Then in September, only a few months later, he bought a cottage on Chapel Lane in Stratford, across from his own New Place home.

In the Reign of King James I

77. King James I Comes to London

ON March 24, 1603, Queen Elizabeth died at the age of seventy. She had reigned for almost forty-five years, and with her death the great Tudor dynasty came to an end. Elizabeth's successor on the English throne was her cousin, James Stuart, King of Scotland (1566-1625). When James reached Whitehall Palace on May 7, 1603, his coming inaugurated a new era in the history of England. James and his successors of the Stuart line were in many ways bad for the country, but they certainly encouraged the drama.

Within ten days of his arrival in London, James ordered a new patent to be prepared by which Shakespeare's company would no longer be known as the Lord Chamberlain's Men, but would come directly under the royal patronage as the King's Men. Shakespeare, Burbage, Armin, Lowin, and the others would continue to perform primarily before the public in their own theatre, the Globe, but the prestige of being known now as the King's Men was a tremendous advantage, and even more than before they were recognized as the preeminent company of the time. As a result, the Globe seems to have become even busier and even more profitable.

78. James I as a Theatre Patron

KING James never, of course, attended a play at the Globe, and neither did Elizabeth before him. The popular conception of royalty's coming to Shakespeare's plays in the public theatre is unhistorical. When the king or queen wanted to see a play, the players would be called to the palace, and would perform there on a specially erected stage.

During the last nine years of Elizabeth's reign, Shakespeare and his fellows of the Chamberlain's company played at court 32 times, whereas between James's accession in 1603 and Shakespeare's death in 1616, the same company did 177 performances at court, more than all the performances of all the rival companies put together. This means that Shakespeare's fellows of the King's Men averaged at least one performance a month at court—or four times more often than they had played there for Elizabeth. In February 1605 James had Shakespeare's *Merchant of Venice* performed twice within a period of three days, so much did he like the play.

79. Queen Anne and the Players

ON OTHER occasions there was a hectic search for plays which the royal couple had not seen, for Queen Anne (1574-1619) was also a great theatrical devotée. Early in the new reign, a prominent courtier named Sir Walter Cope re- ported that he spent "all this morning hunting for players," but without success, and left "notes for them to seek me."

Later in the day, according to Cope's account, "Burbage is come, and says there is no new play that the Queen hath not seen, but they have re- vived an old one, called *Love's Labour's Lost,* which for wit and mirth he says will please her exceedingly." So *Love's Labour's Lost* was sched- uled for the following night.

80. Sir Dudley Carleton

SIR DUDLEY CARLETON (1573-1632), began a steady rise to prominence when James I came to the throne in 1603. From being a member of the first of the English parliaments in James's reign, through a series of important diplomatic posts, he became the principal secretary of state to King Charles I. He maintained a considerable interest in the theatre, and we know from his letters that "on New Year's night [1604] we had a play of Robin Goodfellow" at court. In addition to this performance of *A Midsummer Night's Dream*, we also know from his letters that during the second week of January 1605, plays were presented before the Queen and "a great part of the court." These may have included the performance of *Love's Labour's Lost* which, as we have just seen, Sir Walter Cope arranged with Burbage, but the accounts are not clear as to whether the performance and accompanying feast were held at the house of Robert Cecil, Lord Cranborne, or at that of Shakespeare's old patron, the Earl of Southampton. Such performances attest Shakespeare's professional popularity with the crown and the court.

81. A Highwayman Comments on *Hamlet*

JUST as Shakespeare's high repute with royalty and nobility do not indicate that he hobnobbed socially with monarchs and lords, neither do the references of Gamaliel Ratsey indicate that Shakespeare consorted with highway robbers, though Ratsey was one himself. Ratsey—shown here in the guise of a "wild man"—was a notorious highwayman of the time who was hanged in 1605. After his death, an enterprising publisher issued stories of his exploits, one of which concerned a company of provincial players whom he first paid to act before him and later robbed. As a final gesture of bravado, Ratsey advised the leading actor of the troupe to leave his provincial company and pursue his career in London, where he could compete with "one man" (Burbage?) "to play Hamlet." He proceeded to give other advice, that "there thou shalt learn to be frugal" and "when thou feelest thy purse well lined, buy thee some place or lordship in the country, that growing weary of playing, thy money may there bring thee to dignity and reputation." The final quip about wealth and a country house could refer to Edward Alleyn (see Fig. 23) or Henry Condell as well as to Shakespeare, but the principal interest in the account is that it indicates the breadth of Shakespeare's popularity as a dramatist, which extended all the way from the throne to the gallows.

RATSEIS GHOST.

OR

The second Part
of his madde Prankes and Robberies.

Printed by *V. S.* and are to be sold by *John Hodgets* in Paules Churchyard.

82. Grooms of the Chamber at Somerset House

THE sharers or partners of the King's Company were also Grooms of the Chamber to the King. We do not know exactly what this honor entailed in the way of duties, but we do know that for a period of eighteen days in August 1604 the players were in attendance upon the Spanish Ambassador at Somerset House on the Thames River. The occasion was the peace negotiation between England and Spain, and the King's Men were paid for their attendance. It may be that their assignment was to entertain the ne-

Ciuitatis Westmonasteriensis pars.

the Hall

the Abby

W. Hollar fecit, 1647

83. Playing at Whitehall Palace

gotiating diplomats with plays, though they may have "attended" in other ways. In the course of following his profession, Shakespeare had numerous opportunities to observe the great lords, statesmen, and princes of his time, but it is quite unlikely that he was ever an intimate and accepted member of their circle. His own friends were drawn from among the theatrical people, citizens, yeomen, and gentlemen of London and Stratford.

THE royal palace at Whitehall, just above the city of London on the Thames River, was often visited by Shakespeare and his fellows as they presented plays before the crown. The first notice we have of *Othello* is the payment for a performance at Whitehall on November 1, 1604. Within the next few months, Shakespeare's other plays performed for King James at Whitehall included *The Merry Wives of Windsor, Measure for Measure, The Comedy of Errors, Henry V,* and *The Merchant of Venice.*

84. Actors on Tour

FOR the first year of James's reign, the public theatres were closed because of the plague. This was the first bad epidemic since 1594, and though the worst of it was over by the spring of 1604, there were recurrences in each of the next four or five years. Even when there was no plague, there was usually a little traveling in the summer, but from 1603 to 1609 the King's Men spent more than the usual time on the road. The picture shown here illustrates the arrival of a small touring company at an inn, and also their performance on a temporary stage set up in the street or square. This picture dates from sixty years after Shakespeare's death, but gives a pretty fair impression of touring companies in his own time—except, of course, that there were no actresses in Shakespeare's time, the female roles being played by boys.

85. Shakespeare's London Apartment

FOR the year 1604—and perhaps one or two years before and after—we happen to know where Shakespeare lived while he was in London. It was in the house shown here on the northeast (upper right-hand) corner of Mugle and Silver Streets, located between St. Paul's Cathedral and Cripplegate in the northwest section of London. The house belonged to Christopher Mountjoy, a French Protestant who had fled to England as the result of religious persecutions in his native country. Mountjoy was a well to do maker of women's headdresses, whose daughter Mary was wedded to his apprentice Stephen Belott on November 19, 1604. Shakespeare not

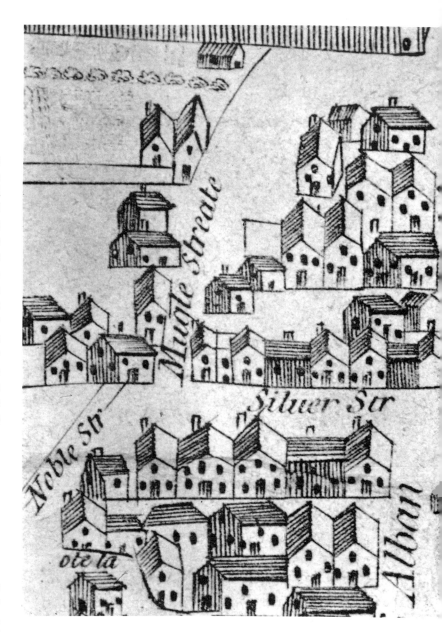

only attended the wedding, but was active as an intermediary between the various parties in arranging the marriage settlement. Eight years later, there was a dispute in court over the financial settlement, and from it we learn of Shakespeare's intimate association with these French Huguenots with whom he lived for a period before and after 1604.

86. Shakespeare Sues an Apothecary

BUT Shakespeare was neither "on tour" nor in the Mountjoy house in London for the entire year. In the spring of 1604 he sold a number of bushels of malt, and later also made a small personal loan, to Philip Rogers of Stratford. Like the man pictured here, Rogers operated an apothecary shop, and in addition sold ale along with pipes and tobacco. Unfortunately he defaulted on what he owed Shakespeare, and Shakespeare could recover his money only by taking court action through his attorney William Tetherton. This is one of the few cases which Shakespeare had to take to a law court. In a very litigious age, Shakespeare, compared to his contemporaries, seems to have been in litigation very seldom.

87. The Welcombe Hills: A New Investment

SHAKESPEARE's own interests continued to revert to Stratford. In July 1605, he made the largest single investment of his life, so far as our information goes, and it included an interest in revenues drawn from the Welcombe Hills, of which this picture affords one view. His initial investment was £440, on which he received a yearly return of £60 according to his own deposition several years later. This represents a price-earnings ratio of 7 to 1, or an annual interest of about 14 per cent, which would not be bad at any time. England's greatest writer may not also have been her greatest businessman, but it is clear that he was very far from being an impractical dreamer.

88. Davenant Tavern and Sir William Davenant

IN his travels between Stratford and London, Shakespeare often broke the trip at the Crown Tavern in Oxford, which was operated by the

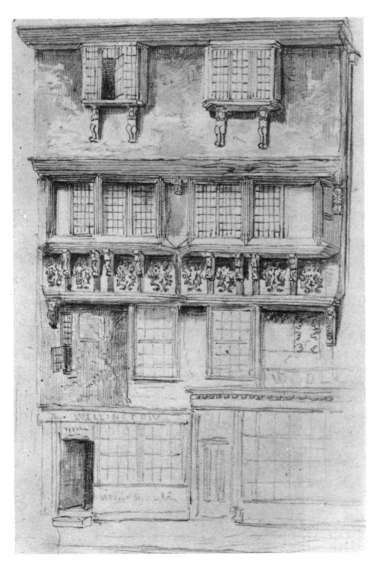

Davenant family. Two sons of this family later recalled Shakespeare's visits: one of the sons, a clergyman, remembered that Shakespeare had given him kisses as a child; the other son, the flamboyant poet and dramatist Sir William Davenant (1606-1668), suggested that Shakespeare's caresses had not been restricted to the Davenant children, but had also been extended to their mother, and that he, William Davenant, was really the poet's bastard son. No one at the time seems to have taken this very seriously, and most seem to have regarded it as reflecting more of Davenant's desire to be thought a second Shakespeare than of the facts of the case in the first place. The two pictures show the family tavern in Oxford, and Sir William, with his nose partly eaten away by venereal infection.

89. William Camden

WILLIAM CAMDEN (1551-1623), pictured here, was Headmaster of Westminster School and one of the undisputedly great historians and scholars of Shakespeare's period. In one of his works published in 1605, Camden names ten writers whom he regards as the "most pregnant wits of these our times, whom succeeding ages may justly admire," and the name of William Shakespeare, along with those of Sidney, Spenser, Drayton, and Ben Jonson, is in the list. Camden had taught Ben Jonson, and the two men maintained a lifelong friendship. It may be that Shakespeare and Camden met through Jonson.

90. Church of England Communion

In Shakespeare's England, men and women were legally required to attend church, and to receive communion. In the spring of 1606 the ecclesiastical court with jurisdiction over Stratford heard the cases of twenty-one persons charged with failure to partake of the sacrament on Easter Sunday of that year, and among those so charged was Shakespeare's eldest child, Susanna. The charges were dismissed after Susanna had appeared and satisfied the court. It will be recalled that Shakespeare's father had been listed for nonattendance at church in 1592 and the reason cited was his fear of prosecution for debt. These are the only instances of the failure of Shakespeare's family to conform to the Church of England during Shakespeare's lifetime, and the records show that neither involved Roman Catholic or Dissenting recusancy. English law strictly required that lists be kept of the names of those who did not attend the Church of England, and there is no evidence, either in London or in Stratford, that Shakespeare absented himself from the services, sermons, and sacraments of the established Church.

91. William Drummond of Hawthornden

DURING the summer of 1606, a young Scot named William Drummond of Hawthornden (1585-1649) came south to London to visit his father, who was a gentleman in attendance on the King. It was evidently during this visit that Drummond, who had recently received his master's degree from Edinburgh University, began to take a lively interest in Shakespeare's works. He mentions having read *A Midsummer Night's Dream*, *Lucrece*, *Love's Labour's Lost*, and *Romeo and Juliet*, and notes that he paid four pence for the latter play. The quarto volume which he bought that summer would today be worth about 50,000 times what he paid for it.

Ben Jonson visited Drummond in Scotland in late December and early January of 1618-1619. Drummond carefully recorded some of Jonson's comments, including the famous remark that "Shakespeare wanted [i.e., lacked] art" as well as Jonson's ridiculing the fact that in *The Winter's Tale* Shakespeare had a "shipwrack in Bohemia, where there is no sea nearby some hundred miles."

92. A Daughter's Marriage

ON June 5, 1607, Shakespeare's favorite daughter, Susanna, was married to Dr. John Hall (1575-1635) in Holy Trinity Church, Stratford. After the marriage, the couple appear to have lived in Hall's Croft, a fine Tudor house located not far from Shakespeare's own New Place. The bride was twenty-four years old, and the groom thirty-two. The year after the marriage, their first child was born, a daughter named Elizabeth.

It was to Susanna and John Hall that Shakespeare bequeathed the bulk of his estate. When their daughter Elizabeth—later Lady Bernard—died in 1670, she was the last of the direct descendants of William Shakespeare.

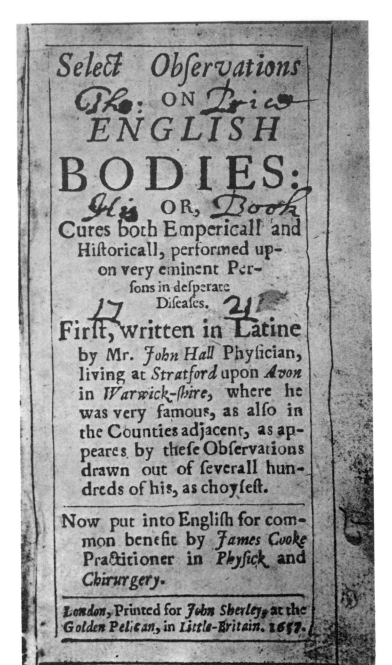

93. A Son-in-Law's Book

SHAKESPEARE'S son-in-law was a doctor, and from all indications a very fine one. His epitaph refers to him as a most skillful physician, and we know that he had a widespread reputation in his profession. Some years after his death in 1635, his medical notebook *Select Observations* was published by a fellow physician. Dr. Hall is said to have been a Puritan, and both he and Susanna were apparently quite devout. Shakespeare seems to have regarded this as a fine marriage.

94. A Brother Buried

SOME months after Susanna's marriage, Shakespeare's twenty-seven-year-old brother Edmund died in London, where he had come to follow his brother into the theatre. We know very little of this young Shakespeare, but his acting career was neither very long nor very distinguished. His burial took place in St. Saviour's Church, pictured here just below London bridge. Also called St. Mary Overy ("Over-the-River"), this was the parish church for the Globe Theatre. The church records indicate an expensive funeral, which could only have been afforded by Edmund's well-to-do brother William. Earlier in the same year, Edmund's illegitimate son had been buried in St. Giles' Church, Cripplegate, just a short distance from where Shakespeare had been living with the Mountjoys.

95. London and Blackfriars

THE left part of this picture shows the Black-friars section of London, just across the river northwest of Southwark and the Globe Theatre. The arrow points to the approximate location of a building about a hundred yards above the Thames River, a building which was quite important to Shakespeare during the last years of his active career. It was the Blackfriars Theatre which he and his partners in the King's Company determined to take over by lease in the summer of 1608. They continued to operate the Globe, but henceforth they had two theatres, the second being entirely enclosed and roofed so that it was suitable for performances at all seasons and in all weathers. Fig. 105 pictures several large buildings, of which one was almost certainly the Blackfriars Theatre, though it must be said that we are not sure which one it was.

The Blackfriars Theatre attracted a more elite clientele than did the Globe or, to put the matter more accurately, the audiences at Blackfriars

FLVVIVS

Varke

were predominantly more wealthy, more prominent, and more sophisticated than the cross section of society which filled the Globe. The fact of all-weather performances, combined with much higher general-admissions prices, meant that the Blackfriars was also considerably more profitable than the Globe. One contemporary estimate placed the gross return at £1,000 per winter more than was customary at the Globe. This may be too high, but it is certainly true that at Blackfriars the King's Men were appealing to a socially choice group, a group which represented only one part of the total audience at the Globe. Henceforth, Shakespeare's plays took on a new cast, more sophisticated, more ethereal and less earthy than his writings had formerly been. This change is noteworthy in the late romances—*Cymbeline, The Winter's Tale,* and *The Tempest*—as Shakespeare the thoroughgoing professional adapted his techniques to suit new opportunities and new demands.

96. An Indoor Stage

WE have no authentic pictures of the Blackfriars interior, and there are still unanswered
questions about some of its features, but the
total dimensions including the stage appear to
have been 66 x 46 feet, with an audience capacity of between five and six hundred. The stage
pictured here does not represent the Blackfriars. It comes from the middle of the seventeenth century, thirty years or more after Shakespeare's death, and the characters on stage are
from many different plays, to represent the
most popular comic scenes of the time. But this
drawing does indicate some interesting things
about the indoor theatres where spectators

could sit to see a play either in the afternoon or
evening. Lighting was provided by chandeliers
hung from the ceiling, and later by rudimentary
footlights at the front of the stage. We know that
torches also hung from the walls, so that the
spectators could follow the action. The atmos-
phere differed radically from the sunlit Globe.

To appeal to their new clientele, the King's
Company began to employ two bright and rising
young dramatists named Beaumont and Fletcher, who had already had considerable success
with the coterie audiences at Blackfriars. Quite
socially acceptable themselves, these two collab-
orators well understood how to appeal to the
sophisticated tastes of the socially prominent
patrons of Blackfriars.

97. Francis Beaumont

FRANCIS BEAUMONT (1584-1616) was the son of Sir Francis Beaumont, Justice of Common Pleas. Educated at Oxford and the Inns of Court, he was a friend of Ben Jonson's, to whom he expressed his admiration for Shakespeare's marvelously clear and "natural" style. In 1613 he married a wealthy heiress and quit writing for the stage. His premature death at the age of thirty-two came a month before Shakespeare's, and he was buried in Westminster Abbey.

98. John Fletcher

JOHN FLETCHER (1579-1625), was the son of a distinguished Church of England clergyman who was successively bishop of Bristol, Worcester, and London. He continued to write for the King's Men after Beaumont's early retirement, and collaborated with Shakespeare in writing *The Two Noble Kinsmen* and a play called *Cardenno*, which has not survived. He is best known for his association with Beaumont, to whom his name is inextricably linked, but the two of them were also influenced by, and in their turn exerted influence on, Shakespeare. The fact that Shakespeare at the height of his success would be willing to learn from these two young men is further attractive evidence both of his personality and of his professional dedication.

Thus thy left hand the Mighty Stagyrite
Supports, that thou might'st shield him wth thy right:
Whose early Soul ay'm'd high, yet allwaies hit;
The sharpest, cleanest, full, square, leading Wit;
The best Tyme's Best; could'st farthest, soonest pierce,
Of all that Walk in Prose, or dance in Verse:
'Tis CARTWRIGHT, in his shadow's shadow drest;
He never is transcrib'd that once writes best.

99. William Cartwright

SHAKESPEARE's last plays were written both for the Globe and the Blackfriars, but they represent an unmistakably new focus, an attempt to write the kind of play which the coterie audience so much admired in Beaumont and Fletcher. Shakespeare's last plays appear to have been very well received, as they certainly deserved to be, but at the same time Shakespeare never completely accepted the new fashions and conventions. The Shakespeare who "pleased all" in the broad cross section of English society at the Globe was less comfortable and, though he was certainly not by any means a failure, he was ultimately less successful with self-consciously sophisticated, blasé, and even slightly supercilious audiences such as those at the Blackfriars.

The changing tastes probably began in Shakespeare's lifetime, but came to fruition only after his death. They may be illustrated in William Cartwright (1611-1643), the Oxford teacher of metaphysics pictured here, who wrote a verse letter to John Fletcher in which he asserted that Shakespeare was both old-fashioned and inferior to his younger successor:

Shakespeare to thee was dull, whose best
  jest lies
I' th' ladies' questions, and the fools' re-
  plies;
Old fashion'd wit, which walkt from town
  to town
In turn'd hose. . . .

100. The Sonnets

SHAKESPEARE's *Sonnets* were published, as this title page shows, in 1609, though we know from Francis Meres's comments that some of them at least were being circulated in manuscript in 1598. Quite evidently, Shakespeare had nothing to do with their publication, and we are not even sure that they follow the order which he had in mind for them. He surely did not proof-read them, and it is even doubtful that anyone else did, so many and so obvious are the errors in this edition. Finally, there is no evidence, one way or the other, as to whether the sonnets were written out of Shakespeare's imagination or about incidents in his life. One thing, however, is certain, as Sonnet XX makes clear: even while writing in the hyperbolic convention of Neo-Platonic friendship, the poet disavowed any homosexual interest in the young man he was addressing. Beyond this observation, the use of the sonnets as a biographical happy hunting ground is a dangerous procedure which can lead equally well to any number of vastly uncertain conclusions.

101. Dr. Simon Forman

ONE of the noted characters in the London of Shakespeare's time was Dr. Simon Forman (1552-1611). Educated at Oxford, and with medical training in Holland, Forman was both a physician and an astrologer, so closely allied were sciences and superstitions at this time. We have no evidence that he knew Shakespeare, but he did know his plays, for perhaps as early as 1610 he had begun to make plot summaries of those which he saw. The earliest of the summaries we know was of *Macbeth*, and like the others it seems to have been intended primarily to preserve a memory of the plot. The doctor's attendance upon Lady Macbeth in the play was particularly impressive to Forman, as a physician. Typical of even the learned men of the time, Dr. Forman was an erratic speller, and in this same short account he spelled "Macbeth" four different ways, while Banquo and Macduff were spelled two different ways—all wrong. This, like the various spellings of Shakespeare's name and indeed all surnames, was quite the usual practice. Forman also saw *Cymbeline* and *The Winter's Tale* (at the Globe) in the spring of 1611, and of the cheating rogue Autolycus in the latter play he wrote what is perhaps the earliest "moralization" of Shakespearean drama: "Beware of trusting feigned beggars and fawning fellows." Only a few months after seeing these plays, Forman died on September 12, 1611, while in a riverboat crossing the Thames. He had earlier predicted this as the date of his death, and there is some suspicion that he took his own life in order to preserve his reputation as an astrologer.

Retirement and Last Years

102. Stratford: the Church and the River

ABOUT 1610 or 1611 Shakespeare returned to Stratford to live. Though the final years of his life were clearly passed in Stratford, we do not know the exact date of his move from London. His cousin Thomas Greene, a lawyer and Stratford town clerk, had been living at New Place for some time with his wife and two small children, and in September 1609 Greene wrote that he had found he could stay on there for another year. This seems to indicate that Shakespeare then planned to return to Stratford in the fall of 1610. In May of 1611 Greene bought a house of his own, and Shakespeare was presumably reestablished with his wife and his unmarried daughter Judith in New Place.

We do not know the reasons for Shakespeare's retirement, but there are several possibilities. It may have been a matter of failing health; men aged more rapidly then than now, and Shakespeare's younger brothers Gilbert and Richard died in 1612 and 1613. Or perhaps he found the new theatre conditions less to his taste and felt the increasing competition of younger and supposedly more sophisticated writers. Or perhaps he simply decided that he had acquired a sufficiently comfortable estate so that he could retire and lead the life of a well-to-do country gentleman. For years he had been investing in property in and around Stratford: it is a charming town, he had always been attached to it, and that in itself is probably reason enough to explain his retirement.

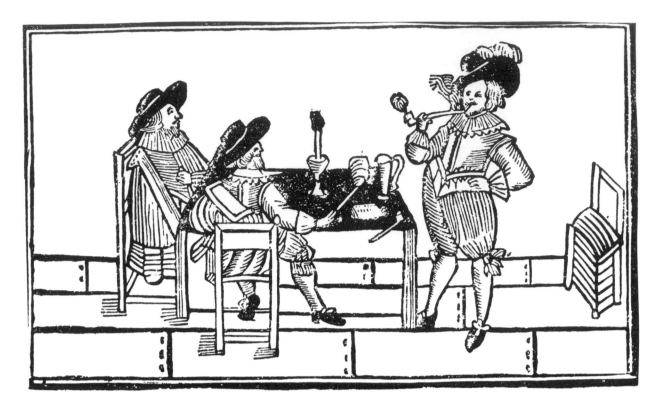

103. Pipes and Ale

WE know of some of Shakespeare's activities in Stratford: he rented out a barn he owned, negotiated with other interested persons on the management of farm lands in which they all had an interest, clarified the title to some of his property, supervised his own estate, and joined with others in supporting a bill to improve the highways. Then, too, there were opportunities for pipes and ale with many friends in the area: the Combe family in the impressive old "College House" in Stratford; Hamnet Sadler, the High Street baker in Stratford and his wife Judith, after whom Shakespeare named his twin children and to whom he left a memento in his will; Thomas Russell, esquire, of Alderminster manor house, who was an overseer of Shakespeare's will, and his wife Anne, whose son Leonard Digges wrote about Shakespeare as a dramatist; his lawyer, Francis Collins; Bailiff Julius Shaw, the merchant who witnessed Shakespeare's will and had a high reputation for faithfulness and honesty; his godson William Walker; and perhaps Sir Henry and Lady Anne Rainsford of Clifford Chambers near Stratford, where Michael Drayton the poet often visited and was cared for in his illness by Shake-speare's son-in-law Dr. Hall. These and other such friends we know he had and valued among the middle class and gentry of the Stratford region.

104. The Prince Palatine and his Bride, Princess Elizabeth

AFTER his retirement Shakespeare returned to London from time to time. On November 1, 1611, his new play *The Tempest* was presented before King James at court. The following spring he was again present in London, this time to testify in a suit involving his old landlords, the Mountjoys, about his recollection of the marriage he helped to arrange in 1604 between their daughter Mary and the apprentice Stephen Belott. The following winter, 1612-1613, saw the King's Men playing frequently at court during festivities honoring the marriage of Princess Elizabeth (1596-1662) to Frederick V (1596-1632), the Elector Palatine, shown here together. One of the most appropriate plays presented at this time was, again, *The Tempest*.

to be sold at the whit horse in pope head
Alley by Iohn Sudbury and George Humble

and William Johnson, the respected and responsible host of the Mermaid Tavern. The papers of sale may indeed have been signed at the Mermaid, where Shakespeare was presumably staying on this visit and again in November 1614 when he and his son-in-law Dr. Hall came up to London once more.

To the right of the Gatehouse is a large building just below the words "black Fryers" on the map. Though we do not know the precise location of Shakespeare's Blackfriars Theatre, it was certainly in this neighborhood and it was probably either this building or one of the other large structures between it and the river. (See also Fig. 95.)

105. A London Investment: Blackfriars Gatehouse

ON March 10, 1613, Shakespeare made his only nontheatrical investment in London of which we know, when he bought the Blackfriars Gatehouse, shown here. The total cost was £140, including a £60 mortgage. The Gatehouse was evidently bought as an investment, not as a home, and was leased out to a tenant. Two of the "trustees" in this transaction were Shakespeare's old colleague and friend John Heminges, who was later an editor of the First Folio,

106. *Henry VIII* and the Globe Fire

EVEN in retirement Shakespeare did a certain amount of writing. One result was the *Two Noble Kinsmen*, which he did in collaboration with John Fletcher and which, probably for that reason, Heminges and Condell did not publish in his collected works in 1623. They did, however, publish *Henry VIII* as his play, and most (though not all) recent scholars accept it as such, contrary to the view of some Victorians that it too was a collaboration. The play was really a spectacular, a series of striking historical spectacles rather than a history play of the earlier type. On June 29, 1613, the performance provided more spectacle than anyone had bargained for, because the firing of an artillery salute to mark King Henry's entrance on the stage set fire to the theatre. Some hot wadding or paper fell on the thatched roof, fire ran all around it like a powder train, and the entire theatre was burned to the ground in less than two hours. No one was hurt in the fire, but according to Sir Henry Wotton, "one man had his breeches set on fire, that would perhaps have broiled him, if he had not by the benefit of a provident wit put it out with bottle ale." The Globe was rebuilt the following year at a total cost of about £1,400, of which Shakespeare as a continuing shareholder would have supplied about £100.

107. Susanna Appeals to Worcester Cathedral

AT about the time the Globe burned, Shakespeare and his family were having their own troubles in Stratford. These concerned Shakespeare's favorite daughter, Susanna, the wife of Dr. John Hall. Though Susanna was evidently a woman of fine character, a certain John Lane spread the slander that she had committed adultery with a local Stratford hatter named Rafe Smith. In July 1613 she brought an action for slander before the bishop's court at Worcester. Shakespeare may well have recalled his own line from *Hamlet*: "Be thou as chaste as ice, as pure as snow, thou shalt not escape calumny" [*Ham.* 3.1.141]. Certainly Susanna did not escape it, but there must have been some consolation in the fact that the consistory court, after inquiring into the case, upheld her innocence and excommunicated her accuser—a favorable conclusion to a very unpleasant incident.

108. John Combe

IN July 1614 came the death of Shakespeare's old friend John Combe, with whom he had been associated for many years. If there is any truth at all in the later legend of Shakespeare's humorous verses describing Combe as a usurer, the verses must have been intended by Shakespeare and accepted by Combe in good humor, for in his will Combe bequeathed Shakespeare £5, which would have been a consider-

The Cathedral Church of Worcester.

J. Harris fecit.

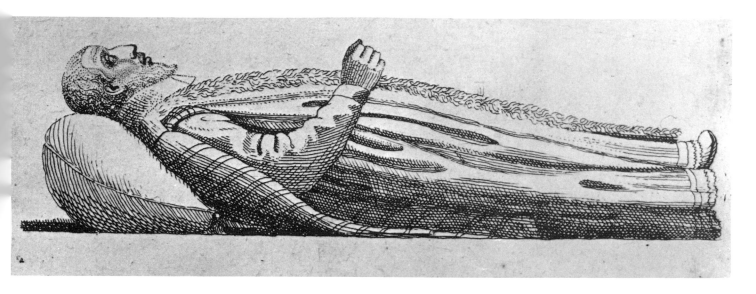

able token of friendship at the time. Furthermore, there is no evidence of a breach of friendship between Shakespeare and the Combe family, and when Shakespeare died he left his sword to young Thomas Combe.

The recumbent statue of Combe was prepared by the same stonecutter, Gheerart Janssen, who later made Shakespeare's memorial bust, both for the parish Church in Stratford.

109. A Thirsty Preacher Visits New Place

DURING the Christmas season of 1614, a visiting clergyman came to Stratford to preach. During his stay he resided with the Shakespeares at New Place, and the town council recorded the fact that it sent a quart of sack and a quart of claret there for his entertainment. Unfortunately the council did not record the name of this visiting preacher, but he was evidently a convivial soul.

We know that other visitors called on Shakespeare at New Place during these years, and that he maintained an interest in his sister Joan Hart and her children, and there were also Susanna and John Hall, and his small granddaughter Elizabeth Hall. But Shakespeare's younger daughter Judith was still unmarried at the age of thirty-one, and when she did marry, it was a match of which Shakespeare obviously disapproved.

Opportunè Importunè

110. House of Judith Shakespeare and Thomas Quiney

ABOUT two months before Shakespeare's death, Judith was married to a local Stratford man named Thomas Quiney (1589–c. 1655) who operated a tavern called the Cage in the house pictured here. The marriage took place during Lent without a license, and both bride and groom were excommunicated. Furthermore, Thomas Quiney appears to have been something of a rake. In a scandalous trial in March 1616, he was convicted of incontinence with a certain Margaret Wheeler, and he had possibly fathered an illegitimate child. Shakespeare's reaction to all this may be surmised from the way in which he changed his will after Judith's marriage. In the final version, the Quineys came off considerably less well than the Halls, and the will indicates a lack of confidence in Thomas Quiney, as well, perhaps, as in Judith herself.

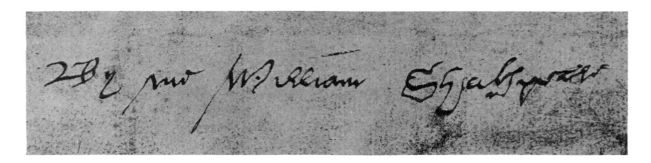

111. Shakespeare's Final Signature

ON April 23, 1616, two and a half months after Judith's marriage, Shakespeare died. The cause of his death is unknown, though some half century after the event it was said that he had "a merry meeting" with Drayton and Jonson, drank too hard, and contracted a fever from which he died. It may be true, but three considerations argue against it. In the first place, Shakespeare's friend Christopher Beeston said that he "wouldn't be debauched and if invited to writ: he was in pain." In the second place, though Jonson was a hearty drinker, Michael Drayton was noted for his moderation. And, finally, some authorities regard Shakespeare's signatures on his will as indicating that he was already a sick man, a month before he died. Again we must say that we do not know. If searches now underway succeed in recovering Dr. John Hall's early notebooks, we may still discover the cause of Shakespeare's death, and much else as well.

112. A Message for Gravediggers

ON April 25, 1616, Shakespeare was buried in Holy Trinity Church, where he had been baptized fifty-two years before. His tomb is beneath the floor, inside the chancel rail, and is covered with a stone which conveys this message:

Good friend for Jesus sake forbear
To dig the dust enclosed here!
Blest be the man that spares these stones,
And curst be he that moves my bones.

The curse is not good poetry, and Shakespeare may or may not have written it, but it speaks a language which every sexton and gravedigger could and did understand. We will understand this inscription ourselves if we observe that Shakespeare's grave was located only a few steps from the door to the old charnel house. This charnel house was literally crammed with old bones which had been removed from their graves to make way for new burials, just as in *Hamlet* the gravediggers moved Yorick's bones to make room for Ophelia. This common practice seems to have horrified Shakespeare (or perhaps it was his family) so much that the curse was carved over his grave. The charnel house itself was torn down about 1800, but Shakespeare's bones have never been disturbed.

A·BOVLSTER LECTVRE.

Dum loquor ista, taces?

Surdo canis.

Will: Marshall. sculpsit.

113. The Second-best Bed?

SHAKESPEARE's wife Anne survived him by seven years, and died on August 6, 1623. She was buried to the left of her husband's grave in the chancel of Holy Trinity Church, below his monument. An unidentified daughter (probably Susanna Hall) placed over her grave an unusually personal inscription. Though the daughter can only provide a tombstone for the mother who gave her life, the inscription reads in Latin, she does pray that Christ will come soon, so that her mother may rise again and join the heavenly hosts.

This indication that Anne Shakespeare was regarded as a good mother by at least one of her daughters tells us almost all that we know about her as a wife. The fact that Shakespeare bequeathed her the second-best bed has of course been the ground for endless speculation. Anne may have nagged at William so much (as a wife

is doing in this satiric cartoon from the period) that he retaliated by making an obviously slighting bequest. But unless we know the full associations of the bed, we cannot possibly be sure that the bequest was intended to be cutting. The "second-best bed" may have been the marriage bed, for example, or it may have been taken from Anne's childhood home, or have had some other pleasant association. We simply do not know, and had best leave the matter at that. At all events, Anne would have been well provided for, with one-third of the income of Shakespeare's estate for the remainder of her life.

114. The First Folio: Shakespeare's Works Then and Now

SOME three months after Anne's death the First Folio edition of Shakespeare's works was registered for publication in London. Shown here on the title page of that edition is the celebrated engraving of Shakespeare by Martin Droeshout. The collar Shakespeare is wearing is one in style during the last five or six years of his life. As Droeshout was twenty-two years old when this engraving was published in the folio, and only fifteen when Shakespeare died, it seems probable that he was copying an earlier portrait, now lost to us. Though Droeshout's work is artistically crude, Ben Jonson hailed it as an excellent likeness.

The purpose of publishing the folio, according to the introductory comments of Shakespeare's editors and old friends Heminges and Condell, was "only to keep the memory of so worthy a friend and fellow alive, as was our Shakespeare," and that statement rings true, as there was at best very little profit in this venture for the editors. They were good men, these two faithful friends, and it is to them that we owe the preservation of half of Shakespeare's plays, including *Julius Caesar, As You Like It, Twelfth Night, Macbeth, Antony and Cleopatra*, and *The Tempest*, to name a few. And what they said in their introductory remarks is as valid today as it was over three centuries ago. They appealed to all kinds of readers, "from the most able, to him

MR. WILLIAM
SHAKESPEARES
COMEDIES,
HISTORIES, &
TRAGEDIES.

Published according to the True Originall Copies.

LONDON
Printed by Isaac Iaggard, and Ed. Blount. 1623.

that can but spell," and invited them to read Shakespeare. And their advice as to *how* to read him will form a fitting conclusion to this biography:

"Read him, therefore, and again, and again. And if then you do not like him, surely you are in some manifest danger not to understand him."

BIBLIOGRAPHICAL NOTE

THE following list provides sources for documenting the biographical information on Shakespeare given in this book, and also suggests a few titles to which the reader might wish to turn for further research on his own initiative. The list is basic and many excellent works have been omitted, but most of the books cited here provide extensive suggestions for further study in various areas of Shakespearian scholarship.

The standard biographical authority is Sir Edmund K. Chambers' two-volume *William Shakespeare: A Study in Facts and Problems* (Oxford: The Clarendon Press, 1930) which may be supplemented, especially for material on Stratford, by E. I. Fripp's two-volume *Shakespeare, Man and Artist* (London: Humphrey Milford, 1938). Levi Fox has provided a brief and interesting history of Stratford in his *The Borough Town of Stratford-upon-Avon* (Stratford-upon-Avon: The Corporation, 1953). Charles Williams abridged the two-volume Chambers' work in *A Short Life of William Shakespeare with Sources* (Oxford: The Clarendon Press, 1933), and Marchette Chute has written a highly readable popular account of the life in *Shakespeare of London* (New York: E. P. Dutton, 1949). A number of scholarly biographies have appeared since Chambers, of which the most up-to-date and comprehensive is probably Gerald Eades Bentley's *Shakespeare: A Biographical Handbook* (New Haven: Yale University Press, 1961). Biographical information discovered since 1961 is introduced into entries 31, 90, and 110, for the first of which readers are referred to my "Shakespeare's Composition of *Lucrece*: New Evidence," *Shakespeare Quarterly* XVI (1965), 289-96, and for the latter two to Hugh M. Hanley's "Shakespeare's Family in Stratford Records," *Times Literary Supplement* (May 21, 1964), p. 441. Most of the known allusions to Shakespeare made during and shortly after his lifetime may be found in the two-volume compilation by C. M. Ingleby and others, *The Shakespeare Allusion-Book* (London: Humphrey Milford, 1932). Among the many works devoted to Shakespeare and the theatre, the following will probably provide most readers with what they want in the way of basic information and understanding: Bernard Beckerman, *Shakespeare at the Globe* (New York: Macmillan, 1963), Gerald Eades Bentley, *Shakespeare and his Theatre* (Lincoln: University of Nebraska Press, 1964), and A. M. Nagler, *Shakespeare's Stage* (New Haven: Yale University Press, 1958). A wealth of general background material on Shakespeare's life and times is to be found in *Life and Letters in Tudor and Stuart England: First Folger Series* (Ithaca: Cornell University Press for the Folger Shakespeare Library, 1962), a collection of illustrated essays written by a number of scholars and edited by Louis B. Wright and Virginia A. La Mar. A very useful dictionary-type handbook is F. E. Halliday's *A Shakespeare Companion: 1564-1964* (Baltimore: Penguin Books, 1964), and an even more extensive work of the same kind has recently appeared under the title *The Reader's Encyclopedia of Shakespeare* (New York: Thomas Y. Crowell Company, 1966), under the general editorship of Oscar James Campbell. A number of distinguished scholars have contributed valuable entries to the latter volume, but the contributions are not equally reliable and some contain surprising errors.

NOTES ON ILLUSTRATIONS

Frontispiece. Portrait engraved by Martin Droeshout for the First Folio, 1623. Folger Shakespeare Library.

1. The Monument Bust in Holy Trinity Church, Stratford-upon-Avon, pre-1623. Folger Shakespeare Library.
2. The Monument Bust, Another View. Holy Trinity Church and Holte Photographics, Stratford-upon-Avon.
3. The Memorial Inscription on the Monument Bust. Holy Trinity Church and Holte Photographics, Stratford-upon-Avon.
4. Unsigned portrait from the time of Shakespeare. National Portrait Gallery, London.
5. Unsigned painting, c. 1720. Halliwell-Phillipps collections, Folger Shakespeare Library.
6. From Richard Day, *A Book of Christian Prayers*, 1578 (Sig. Rlv.). Folger Shakespeare Library.
7. Engraving made in 1769 from drawing by Richard Greene. The first known view. Folger Shakespeare Library.
8. Picture presumably made shortly after removal of plaster. Halliwell-Phillipps collections, Folger Shakespeare Library.
9. From John Amos Comenius, *Orbis Sensualium*, 1685 (p. 256). Folger Shakespeare Library.
10. Drawing by Samuel Ireland for his *Picturesque Views of the Avon*, 1795 (opposite p. 197). The view of New Place in the foreground was taken from a copy of the Treswell drawing reproduced below as Fig. 44. Folger Shakespeare Library.
11. From Alexander Nowell, *A Catechism*, 1593 (verso of title page). Folger Shakespeare Library.
12. From *Elvetham: An Account of Queen Elizabeth's Visit there in 1591*, ed. T.F.R., London [undated, but approximately 1922?] (p. 4), which reproduces the very rare *The Honorable Entertainment given to the Queen's Majesty in Progress at Elvetham, 1591*.

13. This picture is the earliest view I have been able to discover, but it is undated. Halliwell-Phillipps collections, Folger Shakespeare Library.
14. From Henry Holland, *Heroologia Anglica*, 1620 (p. 223). Folger Shakespeare Library.
15. Undated picture from the age of Shakespeare. Reproduced here from Charles Hindley edition of *The Roxburghe Ballads*, London, 1873-1874 (Vol. I, 345). Yale University Library.
16. From G. Franco, *Venetia*, 1626. Folger Shakespeare Library.
17. Detail from facsimile of undated map of London made during Shakespeare's lifetime by Ralph Agas. Reproduced here from J. Q. Adams, *Shakespearean Playhouses*, Boston, Houghton Mifflin, 1917 (p. 213).
18. From *Theatrum Crudelitatum Haereticorum Nostri Temporis*, 1592. Folger Shakespeare Library.
19. Nineteenth century drawing of a typical early innyard. Folger Shakespeare Library.
20. Portrait-cartoon from *Tarlton's Jests*, 1613, based upon an earlier manuscript. Folger Shakespeare Library.
21. Title page of Thomas Kyd, *The Spanish Tragedy*, 1615. Folger Shakespeare Library.
22. Title page of Christopher Marlowe, *The Tragical History of Doctor Faustus*, 1631. Folger Shakespeare Library.
23. Engraving of the original portrait in Alleyn's collection at Dulwich College. Folger Shakespeare Library.
24. Title page of Robert Greene, *Friar Bacon and Friar Bungay*, 1630. Folger Shakespeare Library.
25. Title page of *The Arraignment of J. Selman*, 1611. Folger Shakespeare Library.
26. Title page of John Speed, *Theatrum Imperii Magnae Britanniae*, 1616. Folger Shakespeare Library.
27. From Gabriel Harvey, *The Trimming of T. Nashe*, 1597 (Sig. E2). Folger Shakespeare Library.

INDEX

References are to entry numbers, not pages.